BUILDING A BETTER TEACHER

BUILDING A BETTER TEACHER

Understanding Value-Added Models in the Law of Teacher Evaluation

Mark A. Paige

ROWMAN & LITTLEFIELD
Lanham • Boulder • New York • London

Published by Rowman & Littlefield
A wholly owned subsidiary of The Rowman & Littlefield Publishing Group, Inc.
4501 Forbes Boulevard, Suite 200, Lanham, Maryland 20706
www.rowman.com

Unit A, Whitacre Mews, 26-34 Stannary Street, London SE11 4AB

Copyright © 2016 by Rowman & Littlefield

All rights reserved. No part of this book may be reproduced in any form or by any electronic or mechanical means, including information storage and retrieval systems, without written permission from the publisher, except by a reviewer who may quote passages in a review.

British Library Cataloguing in Publication Information Available

Library of Congress Cataloging-in-Publication Data

Names: Paige, Mark A., 1975- author.
Title: Building a better teacher : understanding value-added models in the law of teacher evaluation / Mark A. Paige.
Description: Lanham : Rowman & Littlefield Publishing Group, Inc., [2016] | Includes bibliographical references and index.
Identifiers: LCCN 2016009887 (print) | LCCN 2016021773 (ebook) | ISBN 9781475807295 (cloth : alk. paper) | ISBN 9781475807301 (pbk. : alk. paper) | ISBN 9781475807318 (Electronic)
Subjects: LCSH: Teachers--Rating of--United States--Mathematical models. | Educational evaluation--United States.
Classification: LCC LB2838 .P335 2016 (print) | LCC LB2838 (ebook) | DDC 371.14/4--dc23
LC record available at https://lccn.loc.gov/2016009887

∞ ™ The paper used in this publication meets the minimum requirements of American National Standard for Information Sciences—Permanence of Paper for Printed Library Materials, ANSI/NISO Z39.48-1992.

Printed in the United States of America

To my family

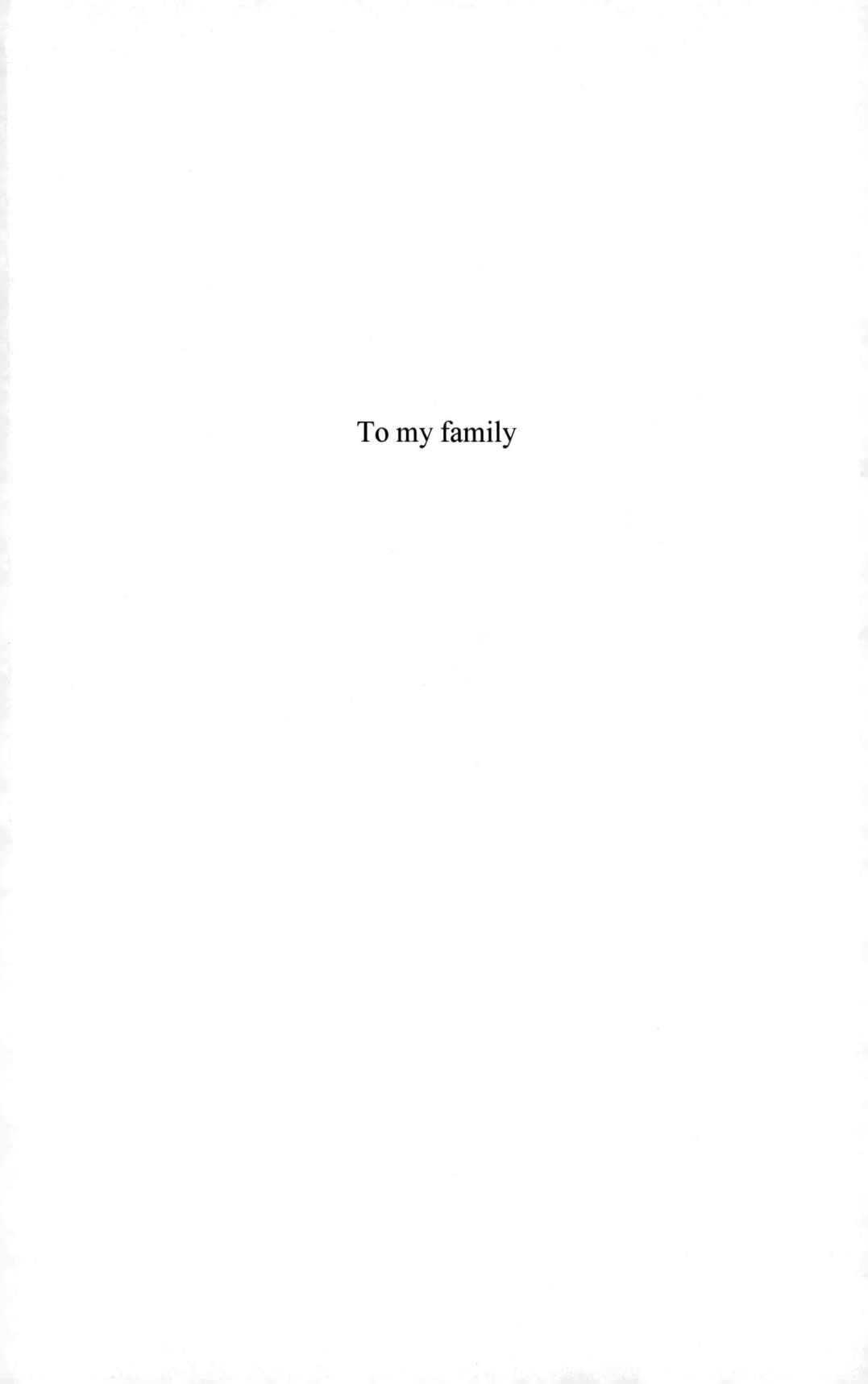

TABLE OF CONTENTS

Preface		ix
Introduction		xv
1	VAMs: What Are They Good For?	1
2	Full Circle: Teacher Evaluation, VAMs, and Employment Decisions	15
3	VAMs Under the Law: Unfair but Rational?	23
4	Pre-Existing Conditions: Legal Deference to School Administrators' Judgment of Teacher Performance	45
5	VAMs, Collective Bargaining, and Arbitration: More Legal Headaches for Administrators?	63
6	Collective Bargaining: A Tool to Mitigate VAM Damage to School Culture	77
7	The Role of Courts in Improving Teacher Quality Through Evaluation	93
8	Lessons Learned: What Policymakers Can Learn from Education Professionals	107
Index		115
About the Author		121

PREFACE

> We have to raise the standards [for teacher evaluation]. We have to help those at the bottom, and if they [teachers] can't do the job, we have to replace them. The only way we're going to reform public education is doing exactly that.
> —Former New York City Mayor, Michael Bloomberg[1]

Our teacher evaluation system is broken. For too long we have enabled poor teachers to remain in the classroom. That almost all public school teachers receive high ratings on evaluations seems, intuitively, absurd. But the consequences are real: poor performing teachers remain in the classroom. For a nation that values educational opportunity, this is an embarrassment. It may even be educational malpractice. How can we tolerate mediocrity in institutions so vital to our democracy as public schools?

Yet there is good news. Education stakeholders recognize these shortcomings. Various constituencies, like teachers unions, school administrators, and policymakers have focused on improving teacher evaluation as part of the larger conversation to improve teacher quality. This is a positive sign. But considerable disagreement remains, especially regarding the appropriate policy design and implementation of teacher evaluation. Opinions diverge regarding *how* we redesign teacher evaluation systems.

Questions at the center of this controversy include the following: What does an effective teacher "look like"? Assuming we can agree on a definition, what evaluation policies will ensure that we have the best teachers in our classrooms? In what ways, if any, can evaluation *laws* facilitate improvement in teacher quality? And, in what ways do proposed evaluation changes raise important legal questions, especially with respect to their use in high-stakes decisions?

Value-added models (VAMs) have engendered substantial controversy in the current discussion regarding evaluation reform.[2] In brief, VAMs are statistical models that attempt to forecast teachers' impact on students' achievement. VAMs, at their core, *estimate* a teacher's impact in this regard, especially on standardized tests. Importantly, these models are premised on the assumption that a teacher causes particular results on tests, and that other variables that may contribute or detract from student performance can be controlled. That assumption is questionable.

VAMs are an alluring elixir.[3] They satisfy our thirst for "data driven" metrics and need to attribute all education results to a school or a particular teacher for accountability purposes. In this regard, VAMs are viewed as a valuable tool in removing poor performing teachers. VAMs allow administrators to identify those teachers that add value and those that do not. Once identified, dismissal is both warranted and supported.[4] That we can evaluate and terminate using data derived from standardized tests—the sine qua non—is irresistible.

But VAMs have fatal shortcomings. The chief complaint: they are statistically flawed. VAMs are unreliable, producing a wide range of ratings of the same teacher.[5] VAMs do not provide any information about what instructional practices lead to particular results. This complicates efforts to improve teacher quality; many teachers and administrators are left wondering how and why their performance shifted so drastically, yet their teaching methods remained the same.

What explains such variations? Specifically, confounding variables outside a teacher's control impact student achievement. Given these drawbacks, the use of VAMs in employment (and in particular, "high-stakes" decisions[6]) has been criticized on fairness grounds. These statistical infirmities raise questions as to whether VAMs can meaningfully contribute to improving teacher quality. Notably, the American Statistical Association (ASA) concluded that they are "unstable" and cautioned against using them for meaningful employment decisions.[7]

In many states, VAMs carry the force of law and *must* be used in high-stakes employment decisions under applicable statutes and regulations. Because of this legal mandate, VAMs have landed squarely in the *law* of teacher evaluation.[8] Thus, the technical and fairness issues raised by policymakers will move from the field of education research to the law. And that is happening; teachers and unions are challenging VAMs under different legal theories and forums.

It is time to step back and consider the consequences of using VAMs, especially in high-stakes employment decisions. That has yet to happen. So far, the singular focus with respect to VAMs has been on their statistical properties and weaknesses. One researcher notes:

> Instead [of practical discussions], what we have is an academic library of hyper-technical reports that discuss value-added in excruciating statistical detail and, at the same time, ignore the many practical realities educators and policymakers face in interpreting and using the measures.[9]

To be sure, understanding the statistical properties of VAMs is important work. But serious gaps exist in understanding the consequences of VAMs as applied in the field.

To date, the practical implications of VAMs—especially those at the intersection of the law—have been overlooked. At best, discussion regarding the law and VAMs—especially as it impacts the ability of administrators to do their jobs—receives a passing reference.[10] This is a striking—and costly—omission. A particular focus on their interplay from a legal perspective is warranted, given the stakes and costs associated with teacher evaluation decisions. This book contributes to a needed conversation about the law, teacher evaluation, and VAMs.

The book makes four conclusions. First, from an evidentiary perspective, VAMs do not strengthen a school district's legal case in contested adverse employment decisions. In fact, VAMs are *entirely unnecessary* to assist a school district in a contested case in court or arbitration.[11] Courts have consistently sustained district termination decisions by deferring to the professional judgment of school officials' regarding teacher performance. Put another way, *courts* do not need VAMs to sustain a termination or other adverse decisions.

Second, because of the statistical flaws of VAMs they actually can *frustrate* school districts' efforts to effectuate a performance-based termination. The statistical questions around VAMs (i.e., whether they are reliable) give plaintiff attorneys an additional line of attack on the wisdom of a district's performance assessments. At the same time, the legal mandates requiring the use of VAMs supplant the school district's most potent evidentiary weapon in defending an adverse decision: a school administrator's professional judgment. In sum, at the very least, the legal requirement of VAMs complicates a school district's case.

Third, VAMs negatively impact school culture, but school administrators may have some tools to mitigate this negative impact. High-stakes accountability—and VAMs—are destructive forces vis-à-vis the creation of a positive learning environment. But this book posits that local administrators and teachers can employ collective bargaining to blunt this impact, to some extent. In particular, the book recommends local stakeholders implement a two-pronged approach: they should employ a specific type of bargaining, interest-based bargaining (IBB), and a specific method of evaluation, peer-assisted review (PAR). The benefits of these models are particularly well-suited to counteract the pernicious impact of VAMs on school culture.

Fourth, stakeholders seeking to minimize the use of VAMs in evaluation and high-stakes decisions should focus their primary efforts in the political realm, rather than on litigation. State legislatures, in particular, are best positioned to roll back the overly prescriptive use of VAMs in evaluation law and policy. Courts, on the other hand, hesitate to overly involve themselves in policy matters, and court action is highly inefficient. Moreover, challenges to VAMs through the federal courts have been unsuccessful; yet political pressure is appearing to have some impact.

To be sure, courts can play an important role in this struggle to reverse some of the misguided policy initiatives that have been embedded in the law. In that regard, litigation should be *part of* an overall strategy. At the very least, legal challenges draw popular attention to the evaluation systems and their absurd results. Moreover, court-based efforts at reform may force political branches to reconcile this dissonance. Thus, litigation may be necessary, but alone is insufficient, in efforts to stop the use of VAMs.

To be clear: this book is not advocating a return to a system of *non*-judgment, where teachers summarily receive positive ratings and the status quo is preserved. Mediocrity should not be tolerated. Evaluations should be linked to best practices and standardized to the extent possible. But, at the bottom line, professional observational judgment of administrators should be the significant, if not controlling factor, in evaluating teachers in high-stakes situations.

PREFACE

In addition: this book is not advocating an abandonment of VAMs in education. VAMs may play some role in improving teacher quality, quite apart from their use in employment decisions. There are different VAMs. Some are stronger than others. Depending on the context, a particular use of VAMs in education may be warranted. The issue of a closely controlled use of VAMs is a question beyond the scope of this book. But it is important to note that VAMs should be removed from any decision to justify and defend adverse employment decisions in a legal forum.

Context matters and it is important to situate VAMs in the current education policy context. In this light, it is essential to remember that many policymakers, especially those in faraway capitals, view education professionals with great suspicion. Indeed, the suspicion borders on total distrust, especially of teachers unions. These forces have driven "reforms" like VAMs that have sought to remove power from local educators and devalue the profession.[12]

But courts do not share this suspicion of education professionals. In fact, at least in the context of litigation, courts value administrators' expertise with respect to assessing teacher quality. Courts appreciate and value precisely what many so-called reformers do not: education professionals may be in the best position to make important personnel decisions and, therefore, we should grant them the freedom to exercise their professional judgment based on years of accumulated formal experience in the field.

NOTES

1. Emmarie Huetteman, "In Washington, Mayor Bloomberg Makes His Case for Teacher Evaluations," *wnyc.org*, January 20, 2012, accessed April 27, 2015, www.schoolbook.org/2012/01/20/in-washington-mayor-bloomberg-makes-his-case-for-teacher-evaluations/.

2. Perhaps representative of the overall debate about value-added models (VAMs), they are also known by other names. In addition, student growth models have been employed in teacher evaluation systems. However, unless otherwise noted, the term VAMs is used here to be all-inclusive.

3. Subsequent chapters outline the issues regarding teacher quality and its relationship to teacher evaluation.

4. The terms "dismissal" and "nonrenewal" have different meanings in a legal sense. Dismissals usually refer to the termination of employment before a

contract ends, or in the case of a continuing contract teacher. Nonrenewal refers to the decision by school districts to simply not offer another term of employment once a contract expires (e.g., a one-year contract for a probationary teacher). Different legal requirements attach to each decision.

5. David C. Berliner, "Exogenous Variables and Value-Added Assessments: A Fatal Flaw," *Teachers College Record* 116, no. 1 (2014), accessed July 7, 2015, www.tcrecord.org/Content.asp?ContentId=17293.

6. High-stakes decisions are those that involve compensation or termination of employment.

7. American Statistical Association, *ASA Statement on Using Value-Added Models for Educational Assessment* (Alexandria, VA: American Statistical Association, 2014), accessed April 8, 2014, www.amstat.org/policy/pdfs/ASA_VAM_Statement.pdf.

8. For a discussion about evaluation and other laws, see Mark Paige and Perry Zirkel, "Teacher Evaluation at the Intersection of Age and Disability Discrimination: A Case Law Analysis," *Education Law and Policy Review* 1, no. 1 (Spring 2013): 72–98.

9. Douglas Harris, *Value-Added Measures in Education: What Every Educator Needs to Know* (Cambridge: Harvard Education Press, 2011), 3.

10. Audrey Amrein-Beardsley, "Value-Added in the Courthouse," April 10, 2015, accessed July 7, 2015, http://vamboozled.com/value-added-in-the-courthouse/.

11. Of course, where VAMs are required by statute, administrators must carefully follow the law and use them. Yet, they should also be sure that, in the final analysis, their opinions form the basis of high-stakes employment decisions.

12. For a discussion concerning criticisms of education professionals and schools of education, see David F. Labaree, *The Trouble with Ed Schools* (New Haven: Yale University Press, 2004), 3.

INTRODUCTION

> His [Andrew Dewey's] example inspired me to have a love for learning and taught me how to accomplish my dreams through organization and determination. He took a big book of dates and names and transformed them into people, thoughts, and decisions that led to the events of history and the world we know today.
> —Brookelynn Russey, upon receiving her degree in aerospace engineering from Texas A&M[1]

Andrew Dewey, a history teacher in the Houston public schools, received a "most effective" rating under his district's evaluation system for the school year of 2011–2012.[2] This assessment, based primarily on his students' standardized test scores, mirrored those from his past seven years.[3] Dewey repeatedly received honors as one of the highest performing teachers in the district over his career.[4]

But in the next school year (2012–2013) Mr. Dewey's rating changed markedly. Despite using the same methods with similar students, his instruction "made no detectable difference," according to the district's rating system.[5] Consequently, the district denied him a bonus. Dewey questioned the validity of the rating. How could an evaluation system reach completely opposite conclusions about the same teacher, using the same methods, and teaching similar students (e.g., same grade, demographic backgrounds)? What did Mr. Dewey do to challenge the evaluation? He sued.[6]

Dr. Sheri Lederman had a similar reversal in fortunes. In 2013, she received an effective rating based on her contributions to students' math and reading state-mandated assessments.[7] During her seventeen-year career she had always been considered effective or highly effective. Her 2013 evaluation placed her in the top tier of her district's teachers.

Yet, in the following year (2014), Lederman received an ineffective rating according to the terms of the VAM-based evaluation system required under state law. This positioned her as one of the *worst* teachers in the district. But, notwithstanding this rating, the majority of her students exceeded state average scores on math and reading tests. Even her superintendent characterized her as an "exceptional teacher."[8] What did Dr. Lederman do to challenge her evaluation? She sued.

At the least, these rating systems seem patently unfair. How can the same teacher be *both* effective and ineffective using the same methods with similar students? Based on such a sensitive rating system, how can we expect a teacher to appropriately modify instruction? More importantly, how is it fair to make significant employment decisions based primarily on VAMs?

Teachers, like Dewey and Lederman, are sure to raise these issues in legal forums. Their cases put the evaluation system on trial. Dewey's and Lederman's cases foreshadow things to come with respect to teacher evaluation challenges in the courts. A growing number of teachers and their representatives have appealed to courts to remedy an unfair—or at least questionable—employment decision based on VAMs. Thus, the shift to VAM-based evaluations for high-stakes employment decisions has raised new legal issues for school administrators and their lawyers.

This book explores the tensions at the intersection of education policy, teacher quality, and the law in seven chapters. Chapters 1 and 2 present the overriding issues of teacher quality and teacher evaluation. Chapter 1 discusses value-added models, presenting their technical and nontechnical issues. Chapter 2 presents the policy debates regarding teacher evaluation and teacher quality and, specifically, the incorporation of student achievement as measured by VAMs as a distinguishing *legal requirement* in state evaluation laws.

Chapters 3, 4, and 5 examine the legal questions that arise because of the shift to VAM-based evaluation systems. Chapter 3 focuses on current lawsuits challenging VAMs, the case of *Cook v. Stewart*, the first federal appeals court decision on the matter, receives considerable attention. A similar case, *Wagner v. Haslam,* also is discussed because they are proverbial "canaries in the coalmine." In both, the plaintiffs (those challenging the use of VAMs) failed. Together, they suggest that *federal* courts may provide little relief for challenges to VAMs.

Chapter 4 demonstrates that VAMs are superfluous with respect to legally defending an adverse employment decision. School administrators already have the power and authority to succeed in court. Existing statutes and authority tilt the scales of justice in favor of school administrators' opinions. In brief, before the introduction of VAMs, the law required courts to defer to a district's employment decision.

Chapter 5 focuses on VAMs in the context of collective bargaining. It notes the case of Washington, DC. In that city's schools, the teachers unions have challenged the implementation of VAMs through arbitration, not the courts. Arbitration is a particular dispute resolution process available under collective bargaining agreements. It has specific attributes that may provide a more favorable forum for teachers seeking to overturn or at least disrupt the use of VAMs in evaluation.

Chapter 6 focuses on the impact of VAMs on school culture. It concludes VAMs defeat the very qualities we need in schools (collaboration, collegiality, shared decision-making) that promote successful student outcomes. Thus, school administrators need tools to mitigate this negative impact. This chapter recommends a two-pronged approach; it suggests that a method of collective bargaining (interest-based bargaining) should be employed to implement a particular method of evaluation (peer-assisted review, or PAR).

Chapter 7 explores ways to secure a complete reversal of our overreliance on VAMs as they relate to employment decisions. Toward this end, there are two institutions available for this purpose: courts and political institutions. It concludes that courts should not be the preferred forum to blunt VAMs. Rather, efforts to curtail VAMs should be primarily channeled to the legislative process. Florida provides an excellent case study for this point. In that state, state officials have reversed their once-abiding faith in VAMs. However, courts can and should play a supporting role in this effort.

Two conceptual ideas frame this book. First, the book borrows from Deborah Stone's observations discussed in *Policy Paradox*. Stone notes that rational policymaking is an illusion. Refined policy ideas (e.g., nicely packaged, almost linear, statistical models that take inputs and translate them into outputs) lead to absurd results when applied in the field.[9] There are unintended consequences, in other words, when policies meet political realities. That's the paradox: sometimes policies that are supposed to improve efficiencies actually complicate matters.

VAMs demonstrate this paradox. On the surface, VAMs appear quite rational. They are complicated models that seek to simply measure the impact of the input on the output. In the field, though, VAMs lead to paradoxical results, such as those demonstrated in the cases of Andrew Dewey and Sheri Lederman. Yet, because districts must, by statute, use the VAM results in high-stakes decisions, the flaws of VAMs are exposed in court. In other words, the collateral issues associated with the fairness of VAMs ultimately frustrate a school district's defense of its decision. In the final analysis, they impede districts' efficiency regarding personnel management.

Second, the book applies a *comparative institutional analysis* to explore a permanent solution with respect to removing the legal mandate of VAMs, at least in high-stakes decisions. This framework examines the relative capacity of the institutions that have the power to change law and policy. In almost all instances, those institutions are: the market, legislature, and courts.[10] Each has capacities and limitations relative to one another and to a particular problem. Courts are better at some things (e.g., protecting the legal rights of minorities) than legislatures. Legislatures are more appropriate in other instances. This analysis presents a question of "imperfect alternatives."[11]

Under a comparative institutional analysis, it has become clear that legislatures should be the primary front for efforts seeking to remove VAMs in evaluation and employment matters. Legislatures are not perfect by any means. In fact, legislative action created the legal requirements regarding VAMs. Yet, on the other hand, courts are not policymaking bodies and, by the same token, are also imperfect. Their recent decisions regarding the constitutionality of VAMs demonstrate a reluctance to review and overturn evaluation statutes, even when they lead to unfair results.

To be sure, courts can—and must—play a supporting role in reforming evaluation policy. In fact, courts can draw attention to the issue and this, in turn, can be leveraged in the political process. Thus, courts play a role in amending the laws of teacher evaluation (and, again, they are in need of change), but they cannot be viewed as the primary means to do this.

The case of Florida presents an excellent case study with respect to the appropriate use of institutions to change policy. As you may know, Florida was an eager and early adopter of VAMs for evaluation and high-stakes decisions. Yet, over the last year, state lawmakers (including those that advocated for VAMs) have removed or diluted the use of VAMs in their state statutes. They have responded to political pressure as the complications of VAMs become more apparent.

No particular ideological or policy agenda motivated this book. To be sure, it started with a suspicion regarding the use of VAMs in employment matters. From my initial perspective, as a former school law attorney and now professor, it seemed that complicated statistical models in evaluation would only lead to a battle of the experts, leaving courts to lean too heavily on experts, rather than the education professionals. At the very least, effective union lawyers would certainly be able to exploit the statistical confusion surrounding VAMs. They could—and are—putting the evaluation system on trial. VAMs have become something of an attractive nuisance in evaluation and employment.

Moreover, there is something intuitively suspect about VAMs in the broader view of education policy. To begin with, they are advertised as yet another "magic solution" to vexing social and policy problems. Common sense suggests that the truth is much more complicated. A healthy skepticism—and close analysis—is warranted in "flavor of the week" policies, especially in education. In terms of a legal analysis, the simplicity and formal neatness that makes VAMs attractive disappears as they are tested in the courts.

To be sure, some state governments are backtracking from their aggressive and prescriptive emphasis on student-standardized tests. Even the federal government, with the passage of the Every Student Succeeds Act, reduced the testing requirements attached to federal education dollars. Moreover, it left teacher evaluation in the hands of state government officials. State and local governments are seeing—and hearing about—the unintended consequences of seemingly rational policies.

Yet even if VAMs are removed or diluted in the context of high-stakes employment decisions, a declaration of victory is inappropriate. Minimizing VAMs does not create better teachers. Resolving the dissonance created by the use of VAMs in high-stakes situations does not end the essential question: How do we evaluate and improve the quality of our teachers?

NOTES

1. "Houston Teacher to Receive Inspiration Award," *Texas A&M Today,* December 15, 2014, accessed April 4, 2015, http://today.tamu.edu/2014/12/15/houston-teacher-to-receive-inspiration-award-2/.

2. Valerie Strauss, "Houston Teachers Sue Over Controversial Teacher Evaluation Method," *The Washington Post,* April 30, 2014, accessed July 1, 2015, www.washingtonpost.com/blogs/answer-sheet/wp/2014/04/30/houston-teachers-sue-over-controversial-teacher-evaluation-method/.

3. Ibid.

4. Plaintiffs' Original Complaint in *Houston Federation of Teachers v. Houston Independent School District,* 2014, 3.

5. See Strauss, supra, note 2.

6. Ibid.

7. Petitioner (Sheri Lederman), Memorandum of Law (2014), 8–9.

8. Ibid., 5.

9. Deborah Stone, *Policy Paradox: The Art of Political Decision-Making* (New York: W. W. Norton Co., 2002), xii.

10. The markets, while relevant in education matters and policy, do not have a direct role in impacting the law of teacher evaluation as it has been constructed with the advent of VAMs.

11. Neil K. Komesar, *Law's Limits: The Rule of Law and the Supply and Demand of Rights* (New York: Cambridge University Press, 2001).

1

VAMs

What Are They Good For?

> He uses statistics as a drunken man uses a lamppost—for support, rather than illumination.
>
> —Andrew Lang, poet

Can a fifth grade teacher impact her students' fourth grade standardized test scores? That was not a misprint; you read that question correctly. Can a teacher essentially *go back in time*? That's impossible, of course. But, according to one scholar's assessment, some value-added models (VAMs) rate teachers based on the past year's achievement of students.[1]

Consider another example. Should a second grade teacher receive an evaluative rating on the standardized test scores of third graders she never instructed who did not even attend her school? In Florida, the answer was yes.[2] In that state, "Teacher of the Year" Kim Cook received an unsatisfactory evaluation for precisely this reason. Florida's evaluations laws (in force at the time), and the district's implementing policies, required such a result. The rating jeopardized her job.

These scenarios are absurd. At the very least, they raise legitimate questions concerning VAMs. How much faith should we place in the statistical models that create these results? Should the employment status of a teacher rest so heavily on such models, as they do now in many states? Moreover, what assurances do we have that VAMs contribute to improving teacher quality?

This chapter explores VAMs in greater detail. It first overviews various value-added models that exist and situates them in their disciplinary roots: economics and statistics. Understanding these disciplinary origins is important; tools designed for one context may not be right for application in another. The chapter outlines concerns that have emerged with respect to the use of VAMs in evaluation and for high-stakes employment decisions. These are examined from a technical (e.g., validity issues arising under VAMs) and nontechnical perspective (e.g., their impact on school culture, etc.).

VALUE-ADDED MODELS: AN OVERVIEW

VAMs purportedly estimate the contribution of a teacher to a student's achievement.[3] The American Statistical Association (ASA) has noted that the goal of value-added assessment (VAA) models "[i]s to estimate the effects of individual teachers or schools on student achievement."[4] Various terms have been used to describe the general idea. These include VAMs (value-added models) but also value-added measurement, value-added assessments (VAAs), value-added analysis (VAA), or simply value-added (VA).[5]

VAMs exist in multiple forms and in complicated formulas.[6] One scholar has identified VAMs in six (6) different forms.[7] These include the following models: gain score, covariate adjustment, layers, cross-classified, persistence, cumulative within-child mixed effects. In addition, so-called student growth models have been distinguished from VAMs.[8] There are distinctions between the two, but they are generally subject to similar analyses in relation to teacher evaluation. Importantly, although the literature has cautioned against using student growth models for purposes of inferring teacher influence, states continue to do just that.[9]

Differences are worth noting among the models. Significantly, some VAMs consider demographic characteristics, and differ with respect to the years of data that can be incorporated.[10] However, all models, like any teacher evaluation tool, are "imperfect."[11] Moreover, there is "no consensus on the most accurate model" because, primarily, the idea of what constitutes teacher effectiveness differs among those models.[12]

VAMs are grounded in economics. Specifically, the production-function model undergirds VAMs. These models attempt to explain the most efficient combination of inputs to reach a desired output.[13] The focus is on productivity and maximizing resources. With this knowledge, resources can be most efficiently deployed to reach an output.

VAMs are a production model primarily deployed by educational statisticians.[14] Theoretically, the transfer of the production-function model to education makes sense, especially in the accountability age. One scholar notes:

> [T]he basic analytical concepts seem applicable to a wide variety of concepts—there is *a priori* no indication that this structure applies to, say, the steel industry, and not the education industry.[15]

VAMs have particular appeal in the current education context focused almost exclusively on results, essentially test scores.

In education, value-added assessments primarily measure outputs in terms of standardized tests. Teachers are the inputs. To be sure, several metrics could measure teacher effectiveness (e.g., graduation rate). But standardized tests are ubiquitous and, accordingly, "the primary emphasis [for purposes of effective teacher evaluation] rests squarely on test-score growth."[16]

VAMs are operationalized with statistical functions. Accordingly, some understanding of statistics is required to deepen an appreciation of the potential and limits of VAMs. The American Statistical Association (ASA) defines statistics as follows:

> Statistics is the science of learning from data, and of measuring, controlling, and communicating uncertainty; and it thereby provides the navigation essential for controlling the course of scientific and societal advance [citations omitted].[17]

Collected data must be interpreted. Interpretation plays a critical role in the use of VAMs. In the case of VAMs, the data is assessed against the ultimate question: does a teacher's VAM score reflect his or her effectiveness? One prominent scholar summarized the issue as follows: "The application of most VAMs involves both intricate statistical methodology and knotty questions of interpretation."[18]

Two competing views exist on how to interpret VAMs captured through large-scale assessments (e.g., state-mandated tests). First, some consider a VAM score as a *descriptive* indicator regarding effectiveness.

The VAM reflects a piece of the overall picture. But, alone, a poor VAM rating is not considered a direct estimate of a teacher's effectiveness. Other evidence or data must be incorporated to make conclusions regarding effectiveness.

Second, others contend that VAMs express a causal link between teacher instruction and student test scores. Under this interpretation, an inference with respect to teacher effectiveness can be made based on VAM scores. If a VAM rating is positive, the effectiveness of the teacher is viewed positively. But if the VAM rating is lower, the teacher's effectiveness is considered lower.[19] This, of course, assumes that teacher effectiveness should be assessed through contributions to student test scores and that a particular VAM model can isolate the impact of other variables on those test scores.[20]

However, there is considerable doubt about the use of VAMs to explain causal relationships.[21] For instance, the leading organization that governs statisticians, the American Statistical Association states: "VAMs typically measure correlation, not causation."[22] In addition, VAMs cannot explain the pedagogical techniques that lead to a particular outcome. Importantly, they are not irrefutable or immune from logical criticism, as cases presented in this book demonstrate.

TECHNICAL ISSUES REGARDING VALUE-ADDED MODELS

Researchers and academicians have focused intently on analyzing technical issues (e.g., the statistical processes and models used) related to VAMs. Studies that have addressed this topic touch on a variety of subjects. These include the use of different types of VAMs that produce contradictory results and the impact of other variables on student test scores (e.g., attendance, among others).

A large portion of the technical debate flows from a central (and disputed) premise of VAMs: that teachers *cause* a student's test score. Indeed, the very term "'effectiveness' denotes a causal interpretation" (think "cause and effect") between the teacher and student growth on tests.[23] Under the typical VAM model, a teacher is assigned a particular numeric value. This value is based on the average growth of their students on standardized tests (in most instances). Their students' growth is compared to the growth of students in other teachers' classrooms to determine relative effectiveness.

Employing VAMs to ascertain causal relationships is problematic. Each classroom is unique and many factors impact student test scores beyond the reach of a teacher's instruction. Henry Braun has stated that:

> The fundamental concern is that, if making causal attributions is the goal, then no statistical model, however complex, and no method of analysis, however sophisticated, can fully compensate for the lack of randomization.[24]

Thus, the general divide regarding VAMs concerns their use in making causal inferences between teachers and student achievement, especially with respect to test scores.

Validity, Bias, and Randomization

Validity issues have been raised with respect to VAMs. A statistical model's accuracy, in great part, is determined by reference to its validity. This link has been stated as follows:

> Validity is the essential consideration in the evaluation of the uses of any assessment. The logical and evidentiary bases for claims and inferences about scores obtained from any testing procedures are captured by a validity argument.[25]

The threshold question is: does the model actually assess what it is supposed to measure? For purposes of VAMs: does a given VAM model actually estimate the impact of a teacher on student test score achievement or gains?

Ensuring validity requires randomization. In a school setting, randomization occurs if "students are randomly grouped into classes, and teachers are randomly allocated to those classes."[26] Preferred assignments would be removed. Randomization would "level the playing field" and teachers could be compared more fairly relative to one another.[27]

Randomization reduces alternative explanations for given results. If we can ensure randomization of teacher and student selection, the inference that a teacher's instruction (not another variable) impacted a student's test score is strengthened. Thus, randomization permits causal inferences. The need for randomization is high, especially for purposes of high-stakes employment decisions based on evaluations.

Yet, without a random experiment the validity of a result is subject to *bias*. Bias, in the technical sense, means that the model we are using (e.g., VAMs) is flawed from a systematic level. Put another way: the model is universally flawed. Most significantly, bias leads to false conclusions, even if the statistical operations of the model are applied correctly.[28]

In practice, classroom sorting is not random.[29] Competing agendas and power drive class composition. Senior teachers, for example, can ensure their classes are populated with high-achieving students. Parents pressure administrators for a particular class placement. Even at the district level, the same concepts apply; teachers seek to teach in schools that are in wealthier neighborhoods.

Academic studies confirm the lack of random assignment in schools and districts. This impact has been particularly acute in areas of high-need students. Less-qualified teachers are disproportionately assigned to teach in high-need schools.[30] Tracking—the systematic grouping of students into particular classes, schools, or clusters—has a long history in the United States education system; notwithstanding criticisms leveled against this practice, it has continued.[31] Schools are segregated based on race and income, both variables that impact student achievement.[32]

In sum, the weight of the evidence suggests that VAMs are inherently biased because of this inability to control for random sorting. That bias is present in VAMs cannot be understated. It calls into question the accuracy of any final conclusions regarding teacher impact on student growth.

Other Factors Impacting VAM Ratings

Out-of-school variables contribute to student performance. First, the most obvious (but overlooked) is the student. Students have different capacities and motivational levels.[33] Students have different aptitudes and abilities formed well before they enter public schools. Notably, a key period of this development occurs between the ages of zero (0) and five (5), thus well prior to when public education begins.[34]

Student demographics influence student achievement. The Coleman Report, once maligned and now embraced, concluded that the socioeconomic status of a student was an overwhelming determinant with respect to the equality of educational opportunity.[35] Other scholars have located the impact of poverty and race on the educational opportunities of children.[36]

Classroom and school composition alter student outcomes. The racial composition of schools impacts student achievement.[37] The proportion of low-performing students in a class has an overall impact on a class's achievement.[38] Other school-level variables impact student outcomes. These include the quality of the school leaders and the resources available at the school, among others.

To be sure, some VAMs claim to account for these variables. However, there are so many—beyond demographics of students (e.g., the compositional and contextual factors above)—that it is virtually impossible to control. One scholar commented as follows:

> Because the number of such variables may be impossible to specify and measure, value-added approaches to judging teacher effectiveness may be fatally flawed.[39]

Additional Concerns: Reliability/Stability (or Noise)

Critics label VAMs as unreliable. VAMs yield unstable results from year to year.[40] For instance, one study characterized value-added estimates as only moderately reliable from year to year.[41] The choice of model impacts the stability of outcomes.[42] Moreover, the problems of stability are interrelated with that of bias (e.g., nonrandom assignment of teachers); different models generate different rankings due to the type of students in respective classrooms.[43]

In sum, technical criticisms of VAMs arise at various levels in the literature. In particular, VAMs are considered flawed because they cannot provide for randomization, they create bias, and they are generally unreliable. Together, these issues cast doubt about their ability to determine any causal link between student test scores and particular teachers.

NONTECHNICAL CONCERNS

There are also "nontechnical" questions regarding VAMs. To date, much of the discussion has been focused on technical issues of VAMs. However, literature in this area is developing, but a cursory view of prevailing themes is discussed below.

Improving Teacher Quality

The essential nontechnical criticism of VAMs is this: how, if at all, do they contribute to teachers' understanding of their practice? Unfortunately, the answer is not generally known. Indeed, VAMs are summative ratings. They contribute to an overall rating ("effective" or "ineffective," etc.), but they do not provide particularly important information about what types of practice contributed to this rating. Thus, even assuming they are accurate, they do not answer significant instruction-related questions that might help the teacher reframe or improve his or her teaching.

To be sure, VAMs are not designed to achieve this explanatory result. Their purpose is summative. Yet it is important to note this deficiency. Thus, to the extent that we seek to use teacher evaluation systems to improve practice, VAMs play a limited role, at least with respect to providing actionable information. Moreover, this lack of information contrasts with other evaluation systems that have a formative component and that are closely linked to traits we relate to teacher effectiveness.[44]

Emphasis on Tests

Because VAMs emphasize standardized tests, they also raise parallel concerns associated with high-stakes accountability. VAMs elevate the significance of standardized tests and testing in general. This focus raises a number of issues as they relate to the unintended consequences of VAMs. To begin with, there is considerable disagreement about the overreliance on tests and the stress that this may be causing many children, especially at an early age. The reliance on VAMs ensures that standardized tests will remain prominent in our education system and, by extension, so will the continued (and growing) resistance to their use.

In addition, VAMs define "effective teachers" narrowly. Indeed, as discussed above, there are many ideas about defining and assessing teacher effectiveness. Yet, when we employ VAMs, the message is clear that we prefer one definition: the one that elevates performance on standardized tests and, at the least, tests in general (as opposed to building critical thinking skills or developing given artistic talents).

The narrow focus on tests, in turn, limits school curricula. Because of this shift, resources and attention have become narrowly diverted to the test areas, in particular math and reading. Non-tested subjects (e.g., art and music) are devalued. VAMs continue this winnowing and, in the process, limit the goals of public education.

KEY POINTS

- VAMs are statistical models that attempt to *estimate* a teacher's contribution to student achievement.
- There are at least six (6) different VAMs, each with relative strengths and weaknesses.
- VAMs rely heavily on standardized tests to assess student achievement.
- VAMs have been criticized on a number of grounds as offending various statistical principles that ensure accuracy. Scholars have noted that VAMs are biased and unstable, for example.
- VAMs originated in the field of economics as a means to improve efficiency and productivity.
- The American Statistical Association has cautioned against using VAMs in making causal conclusions between a teacher's instruction and a student's achievement as measured on standardized tests.
- VAMs raise numerous nontechnical issues that are potentially problematic to the health of a school or learning climate. These include the narrowing of curriculum offerings and a negative impact on workforce morale.

NOTES

1. Jesse Rothstein, "Teacher Quality in Educational Production: Tracking, Decay, and Student Achievement," *Quarterly Journal of Economics* 125, no. 1 (2010): 175–214: 175.

2. *Cook v. Stewart*, 28 F. Supp. 3d 1207 (N.D. Fla. 2014).

3. Stuart Yeh, "The Reliability, Impact, and Cost-Effectiveness of Value-Added Teacher Assessment Methods," *Journal of Education Finance* 37, no. 4, (2012): 374–399: 399, 374. VAMs have been used to estimate the effectiveness of other educational factors, like schools. However, for purposes of this discus-

sion, the focus is on the use of VAMs to estimate the impact or contribution of a teacher on a student's test score.

4. *ASA Statement on Using Value Added Models for Educational Assessment* (American Statistical Association, April 8, 2014), accessed June 1, 2015, www.amstat.org/policy/pdfs/ASA_VAM_Statement.pdf.

5. Kevin Schaaf and Daniel Dockterman, "VAM in Greek, English, and Implication: Explanations of Different Models and Their Effects on Aggregate and Individual Teacher Outcomes," *Interactions: UCLA Journal of Education and Information Studies* 10, no. 1 (2014): 1–27: 2.

6. Ibid. It is interesting to note that there has been little attention on these different models until relatively recently.

7. Edward Wiley, *A Practitioner's Guide to Value Added Assessment* (Boulder, CO: National Education Policy Center, January 1, 2006), accessed July 5, 2015, http://nepc.colorado.edu/publication/a-practitioners-guide-value-added-assessment-educational-policy-studies-laboratory-resea.

8. Daniel Goldhaber, Brian Gabele, and Joe Walch, "Does the Model Matter? Exploring the Relationship Between Different Student Achievement-Based Teacher Assessments," *Statistics and Public Policy* 1, no. 1 (2014): 29. For purposes of teacher evaluation, the terms "VAM" and "student growth models" have been used interchangeably. See, for example, Michelle Croft and Richard Buddin, 44 J.L. & Educ. 1 (2015) (referring interchangeably to the concepts of VAMs and student growth in their discussion concerning statistical models to assess teacher outputs in terms of standardized tests and other measures). Unless otherwise noted, going forward, the term "VAM" shall be used to refer to both models.

9. See also, Bruce Baker, "Take Your SGP and VAMit, Damn It!" *School Finance* 101, September 2, 2011, accessed March 25, 2015, https://schoolfinance101.wordpress.com/2011/09/02/take-your-sgp-and-vamit-damn-it/ (summarizing the conflation of SGP and VAMs in relation to their use on teacher evaluation systems). See also, Dan Goldhaber, Joe Walch, and Brian Gabele, supra, note 8, at 29 (noting that in practice SGPs are used to make causal inferences about student and classroom growth, even though they are not designed for such purpose).

10. Wiley, supra, note 5, at 5.

11. Ibid.

12. Schaaf and Dockterman, note 5, at 4.

13. Wiley, *A Practitioner's Guide*, 6. See also, Douglas Harris, "Would Accountability Based on Teacher Value Added Be Smart Policy? An Examination of the Statistical Properties and Policy Alternatives," *Journal of Education Finance and Policy* 4, no. 4 (Fall 2009): 319–350: 321.

14. Harris, supra, note 13, at 321.

15. Eric Hanushek, "Conceptual and Empirical Issues in the Estimation of Educational Production Functions," *Journal of Human Resources* 14, no. 3 (1979): 351–88: 353.

16. Sean Corcoran, "Can Teachers be Evaluated by their Students' Test Scores: Should They Be? *Education Policy for Action Series* (Providence, RI: Annenberg Institute for School Reform, 2010), accessed July 5, 2015, http://annenberginstitute.org/pdf/valueAddedReport.pdf, 3.

17. *American Statistical Association: What Is Statistics* (Virginia: American Statistical Association, 2015), accessed July 1, 2015, www.amstat.org/careers/whatisstatistics.cfm.

18. Henry Braun, "Using Student Progress to Evaluate Teaching: A Primer on Value-Added Models" (Princeton, NJ: Policy Information Center, Educational Testing Service, 2005): 1–16: 7.

19. It is worth noting that effectiveness in the context of VAMs is a relative term, comparing teachers' contributions against colleagues.

20. Derek Briggs, "Making Value-Added Inferences from Large-Scale Assessments," in *Improving Large-Scale Assessment in Education: Theory, Issues, Practice*, eds. Marielle Simon, Kadriye Ercikan, Michel Rousseau (London: Routledge Press, 2013).

21. Rothstein, supra, note 1, at 176.

22. *ASA Statement on Using Value-Added Measures for Educational Assessment,* (American Statistical Association, April 8, 2014), accessed June 1, 2015, www.amstat.org/policy/pdfs/ASA_VAM_Statement.pdf.

23. Henry Braun, supra, note 18, at 8.

24. Ibid.

25. Haggai Kupermintz, "Teacher Effects and Teacher Effectiveness: A Validity Investigation of the Tennessee Value Added Assessment System," *Educational Evaluation and Policy Analysis* 25, no. 3 (Fall 2003): 287–98: 288.

26. Braun, supra, note 18, at 3.

27. Ibid.

28. Sarah Boslaugh and Paul Andrew Watters, *Statistics in a Nutshell* (Cambridge: O'Reilly, 2008), 15.

29. Arguably, they should not be. Some teachers should be paired with particular teachers based on individualized considerations. A hallmark of instruction relates to how well a teacher can accommodate the needs of students, both intellectually and emotionally. Careful consideration should be paid to this relationship that random assignment would completely miss.

30. Charles T. Clotfelter, Helen F. Ladd, and Jacob L. Vigdor, "Teacher-Student Matching and the Assessment of Teacher Effectiveness," *Journal of Human Resources* XLI, no. 4 (Fall 2006): 778–820: 778.

31. See generally, Adam Gamoran, Martin Nystrand, Mark Berends, and Paul C. LePore, "An Organizational Analysis of the Effects of Ability Grouping," *American Educational Research Journal* 32, no. 4 (Winter 1995): 687–715.

32. To be sure, some suggest that the randomization argument may be overblown. One study found that a teacher's value-added measures calculated in a randomized setting were accurate in a nonrandom setting in subsequent years. See Thomas Kane and Douglas Staiger, "Estimating Teacher Impacts on Student Achievement: An Experimental Evaluation," (NBER Working Paper Series 14607, December 2008) accessed January 3, 2015, www.nber.org/papers/w14607. The study, however, had a small sample size and teachers included were selected by school principals.

33. Some might suggest that this comment reflects an "excuse" for different student outcomes. Yet it should be noted that the education literature and research consistently recognize that children have individual needs and differences.

34. *The Foundations of Lifelong Learning Are Built in Early Childhood* (Cambridge, MA: National Scientific Council on the Developing Child, 2010), accessed April 23, 2015, http://developingchild.harvard.edu/resources/reports_and_working_papers/foundations-of-lifelong-health/.

35. James Coleman, et al., *Equality of Educational Opportunity Study* (Washington, DC: United States Department of Health, Education, and Welfare, 1966), i–737.

36. See, for example, Richard Rothstein, "Why Children from Lower Socioeconomic Classes, on Average, Have Lower Academic Achievement Than Middle Class Children," *Closing the Opportunity Gap: What America Must Do to Give Every Child an Even Chance*, eds. Prudence L. Carter and Kevin G. Welner (New York: Oxford University Press, 2013): 61–76.

37. See, for example, Gary Orfield, "Housing Segregation Produces Unequal Schools: Causes and Solutions," *Closing the Opportunity Gap: What America Must Do to Give Every Child an Even Chance,* eds. Prudence L. Carter and Kevin G. Welner (New York: Oxford University Press, 2013): 40–60.

38. Caroline Hoxby, "Peer Effects in the Classroom: Learning from Gender and Race Variation" (Cambridge, MA: National Bureau of Economic Research, NBER Working Paper 7867, 2000).

39. David C. Berliner, "Exogenous Variables and Value-Added Assessments: A Fatal Flaw," *Teachers College Record* 116, no. 1 (2014): 18.

40. See, generally, Sean Corcoran and Dan Goldhaber, "Value Added and Its Uses: Where You Stand Depends on Where You Sit," *Education Finance and Policy* 8, no. 3 (Summer 2013): 418–434: 426.

41. Daniel F. McCaffrey, Tim R. Sass, J. R. Lockwood, and Kata Mihaly, "The Intertemporal Variability of Teacher Effect Estimates," *Education Finance and Policy* 4, no. 4 (2009): 527–606: 572

42. Dan Goldhaber, Pete Goldschmidt, and Fannie Tseng, "Teacher Value-Added at the High School Level: Different Models, Different Answers?" *Educational Evaluation and Policy Analysis* 35, no. 2 (June 2013): 220–36: 220.

43. Dan Goldhaber, Joe Walch, and Brian Gabele, "Does the Model Matter? Exploring the Relationship Between Different Student Achievement-Based Teacher Assessments," *Statistics and Public Policy* 1, no. 1 (2014): 28–39: 28.

44. Charlotte Danielson, "Teacher Evaluation: What's Fair? What's Effective? Observing Classroom Practice," *Educational Leadership* 70, no. 3 (2012): 32–37: 37.

2

FULL CIRCLE

Teacher Evaluation, VAMs, and Employment Decisions

> I think 50 percent [of an evaluation] based on tests is too much. We need a human touch any time we evaluate anyone for anything.
> —Carmen Fariña, Chancellor of the New York City Schools [1]

In 2014, a state trial court judge ruled that the California legislature failed to provide students an adequate education under the state's constitution because of statutes that perpetuated poor teaching quality.[2] More specifically, the plaintiffs argued that state tenure and reduction in force (RIF) statutes allowed "grossly ineffective" teachers to remain in classrooms.[3] The case—*Vergara v. State*—has become well known in policy and legal circles. The core issue concerned teacher quality and its relationship to the law.

Beatriz Vergara, a student-plaintiff in the case, testified about characteristics of a poor teacher. In particular, she cited her sixth grade math teacher.[4] This teacher could not control the class. The room was "loud." Vergara could not concentrate. This incompetence led to poor performance on high-stakes tests. She attributed her low score on math assessments and subsequent placement in a remedial math class for seventh grade to her teacher's shortcomings. In sum, Vergara's definition of a high-quality teacher related directly to her performance on tests.

Numerous experts that testified concurred with this definition. A Harvard economist testified that teachers with high value-added ratings, primarily assessed with reference to standardized tests, contributed to the long-term success of their students (e.g., higher earning power, post-secondary academic achievement).[5] To be sure, many variables impact teacher quality. These include: educational background, empathy, years of experience, and the ability to implement best instructional practices. But, as the *Vergara* case suggests, a definition that prominently features test scores was adopted by the courts.

Recent changes to teacher evaluation systems mirror this emphasis. The federal government, through Race to the Top Fund, offered significant financial incentives that encouraged states to link evaluation laws and regulations to standardized test achievement. Consequently, many states amended their evaluation laws *and* related employment laws (e.g., tenure) to require that student achievement on tests be a prevailing feature of a teacher's evaluation.

In total, approximately two-thirds of states enacted some form of teacher evaluation reforms along these lines.[6] Because most states require the use of VAMs (and at least student achievement), VAMs themselves play an important role in employment decisions. The shift to VAMs impacts high-stakes employment decisions and, importantly, the defense of those decisions in a legal forum. Thus, the connection between the law, VAMs, evaluations, and employment decisions is complete.

The chapter explores these links and is organized as follows. It first discusses the legal and policy initiatives that set the current accountability context: No Child Left Behind Act of 2001 (NCLB) and Race to the Top Fund (RttT), respectively. It notes how they have defined teacher quality and, in the case of RttT, required the use of student achievement in assessing teachers. The chapter notes the centrality of VAMs in state evaluation laws and regulations. Readers should see how the various legal mechanisms—beginning at the federal and state levels—have defined the current form of teacher evaluation and its reliance on student test scores.

THE LEGAL SOURCES OF VAM-BASED EVALUATIONS

The accountability emphasis on standardized tests resulted from two recent legal mechanisms. First, in 2001, No Child Left Behind (NCLB) focused squarely on test-based educational outputs. For instance, schools or districts that could not demonstrate some degree of progress on their standardized test scores would be sanctioned under terms of the law.[7]

Most notably, that law ambitiously called for all students to demonstrate proficiency by 2014.[8] Thus, since 2000, test score performance has been embedded in education law.

Second, Race to the Top went a logical step further. It linked teacher evaluation to student achievement on state-mandated tests.[9] It set forth a prescriptive regimen to effectuate this connection.[10] RttT defined student achievement with explicit reference to standardized state assessments. Under governing regulations, student achievement is defined as follows:

a. For those **subjects tested under state-mandated tests**, student achievement is defined as: (1) a student's score on the state assessments and, as appropriate, (2) other measures of student learning, provided they are rigorous and comparable across classrooms.
b. For **non-tested grades and subjects**: Alternative measures of student learning and performance, such as student test scores on pre-tests and end-of-course tests; student performance on English language proficiency assessments; and other measures of student achievements that are rigorous and comparable across classrooms.[11]

In addition, the applicable regulations define "student growth" as the "change in student achievement for an individual student between two or more points in time."[12]

The regulations combine the terms student achievement and growth to rate teacher effectiveness. For instance, an "effective teacher" is defined as one whose students achieve "acceptable rates" of student growth, as that term is defined above.[13] A highly effective teacher is defined as one whose students achieve "high rates" of growth (e.g., one-and-a-half grade levels in an academic year).[14] Thus, teachers who instruct in state-mandated tested areas, such as math and reading, will have their summative ratings linked, in some degree, to student test scores if RttT applies in their state.

A Sampling of State Use of Student Achievement in Teacher Evaluation

A window into Florida provides an excellent example of how RttT has trickled into state evaluation laws. That state's teacher evaluation statute reads as follows:

> Performance of students—At least one-third of a performance evaluation must be based upon data and indicators of student performance . . . [and] must include growth or achievement data of the teacher's students.[15]

The statute defines appropriate measures of student performance. It notes that the state commissioner of education must develop a formula for assessing student performance on two subjects—English language and mathematics.[16]

The state of Florida maintains a value-added score system for teachers who instruct in subjects that have a statewide assessment.[17] For those teachers that instruct in subjects not tested by a statewide assessment, local school districts must develop an "equally appropriate" formula.[18]

Other states have adopted similar statutory and evaluation regulations, subject to some slight variations.[19] Tennessee, for example, requires that 30 percent of an evaluation be comprised of "student achievement measures."[20] The statute further requires that 15 percent of this evaluation must be based on the TVAAS (Tennessee Value-Added Assessment System) measures, where applicable (e.g., for teachers instructing in standardized tested areas, like math and reading).[21]

Massachusetts requires an educator's evaluation consist of two "student performance measures"; for those teachers instructing in state-tested subjects (e.g., math and reading), the state standardized tests must be one of these measures.[22] Massachusetts does not specify what portion of the evaluation must be based on growth measures in standardized tested areas. Regardless, those measures *must* be considered. As of 2013, thirty-five states used student achievement in their teacher evaluation regulations and laws.[23]

Educator Evaluation, Test Scores, and Teacher Employment

State laws also now link teacher evaluations (again, in many instances reliant on VAMs) to employment decisions. Florida law, again, demonstrates this connection. In that state, salary adjustments are now connected to teacher evaluations.[24] In Massachusetts, tenure (or professional teacher status, the term used in that state) can be achieved only when a teacher received ratings related to the state's evaluation system.[25] The point is this: significant employment decisions are now linked to evaluation systems that rely on student test performance.

The trend to link teacher to employment decisions is national. For example, a 2013 study found the following:

- forty-one states require some "objective" measure of student performance;
- twenty states required that "student growth" be the "preponderant criteria"; and
- nineteen states linked tenure to evaluation ratings.[26]

To be sure, some states have retrenched. Florida and Tennessee—once "leaders" in adopting tight links between test scores, evaluation, and employment—have reduced the amount of a VAM rating required to be part of a teacher's evaluation. Originally, Florida and Tennessee both required that a teacher's evaluation consist of at least 50 percent of this measure.

Regardless of some slight retractions, VAMs appear to be here to stay. One research study speculated as follows:

> [W]e suspect that such reforms are here to stay and that test-based measures of teacher performance will be incorporated into teacher evaluation systems with increasing frequency.[27]

Thus, the problems—both legal and otherwise—that VAMs introduce will also remain.[28]

However, legally requiring VAMs in employment decisions is problematic. Specifically, the requirement minimizes local officials' ability to "ground truth" their results and prevent absurd results. As scholar Henry Braun notes:

> [L]egislation inflexibly determine[s] the indicators to be employed and how they are to be combined without much regard to either the quality

of the underlying data or to the statistical properties of the composite rating.[29]

The complications caused by this inflexibility are explored in the following chapters. What is clear, however, is that in recent years VAMs have been secured as legal requirements not just in evaluating teachers, but also in making significant, high-stakes decisions.

KEY POINTS

- Student achievement is predominantly viewed as performance on standardized tests.
- Many policymakers assume that teacher quality is best assessed with reference to student achievement on standardized tests.
- Federal and state governments have encouraged the use of VAMs in teacher evaluation laws and regulations. Thus, VAMs have the force of law.
- In recent years, state legislatures have adopted numerous laws explicitly linking teacher evaluation to significant employment decisions, such as termination or bonuses. Thus, as a matter of law, VAMs must be incorporated into these high-stakes decisions.
- Mandated use of VAMs for the purposes of high-stakes decisions will likely cause problems for administrators as they implement evaluation regimens in future years.

NOTES

1. Elizabeth Harris, "New York City Schools Chancellor Objects to Cuomo's Plan for Grading Teachers," *The New York Times*, February 3, 2015, accessed June 24, 2015, http://mobile.nytimes.com/2015/02/04/nyregion/new-york-city-schools-chancellor-objects-to-cuomos-plan-for-grading-teachers.html?_r=0.
2. *Vergara v. State of California*, No. BC484642 (Cal. Sup. Ct., Aug. 27, 2014) (unpublished decision).
3. Ibid. at 8.
4. "Testimony of Beatriz Vergara," accessed June 25, 2015, https://vimeo.com/86567820.

5. "Testimony of Dr. Raj Chetty," accessed June 25, 2015, https://vimeo.com/85786192.

6. National Conference of State Legislatures, "Evaluating Effective Teachers," *NCSL* (2013), accessed November 20, 2015, www.ncsl.org/research/education/evaluating-effective-teachers635188303.aspx, accessed November 20, 2015.

7. *No Child Left Behind Act of 2001*, PL 107–110 § 1116 et seq.

8. Ibid. at § 1111(b)(2)(F).

9. It is understood that Race to the Top employs the term "student achievement" to include achievement in areas outside of those subject to state standardized tests. But it also required that, where possible, such achievement be assessed under terms of state-mandated assessments. These tests, by virtue of NCLB, occur in math and reading, at a minimum.

10. "State Requirements for Teacher Evaluation Policies Promoted by Race to the Top," *NCEE Evaluation Brief* (National Center for Education Evaluation and Regional Assistance, Institute of Education Sciences, 2014), 2, accessed May 12, 2015, http://files.eric.ed.gov/fulltext/ED544794.pdf.

11. U.S. Department of Education, "Race to the Top Fund," *Federal Register* 74, no. 221 (November 18, 2009): 59836–59872, 59840.

12. Ibid. at 58939.

13. Ibid., note 11.

14. Ibid.

15. Fla. Stat. Ann. § 1012.34(3)(a)(1).

16. Ibid. at § 1012.34(3)(7)(a) (defining "measurement of student performance" for purposes of evaluation).

17. Ibid.

18. Ibid.

19. Although not exhaustive, this list includes Tennessee, Massachusetts, and Colorado, among others.

20. Tennessee State Board of Education, Teacher and Principal Evaluation Policy 5.201 (Revised 1/29/2016).

21. It is worth noting, and discussed later, that Tennessee has reduced this requirement. Initially, the state required that 35 percent of an evaluation be based on TVAAS measures, where applicable.

22. Massachusetts Department of Elementary and Secondary Education, Education Laws and Regulations, "Evaluation of Educators," 603 CMR 35.09(2)(a)(1) (regulation requiring use of the state standardized test "MCAS . . . where available" as one of the two measures of a teacher's impact on student learning).

23. Kathryn M. Doherty and Sandi Jacobs, "State of the States 2013: Connect the Dots: Using Evaluations of Teacher Effectiveness to Inform Policy and Practice," National Council on Teacher Quality.

24. Fla. Stat. Ann. § 1012.22(1)(c)(5).

25. Massachusetts Department of Elementary and Secondary Education, 603 CMR 35.09(2)(a)(1) and 35.08(6) (2014).

26. Doherty and Jacobs, supra, note 24, at i.

27. Dale Ballou and Matthew Springer, "Using Student Test Scores to Measure Teacher Performance: Some Problems in the Design and Implementation of Evaluation Systems," *Educational Researcher* 44, no. 2 (March 2015): 77–86: 77.

28. It is worth repeating that VAMs may have a role in education and, *perhaps* evaluation. The book takes no position on the future development of VAMs. Yet, the central tenet of the book remains as follows: Because of their statistical flaws, VAMs should not be used in either important evaluation processes or in employment matters. Their risks (e.g., wrongly identifying poor performing teachers and jeopardizing their employment) far outweigh any benefit in such high-stakes situations.

29. Henry Braun, "The Value in Value Added Depends on the Ecology," *Educational Researcher* 44, no. 2 (March 2015): 127–131: 129.

3

VAMs UNDER THE LAW

Unfair but Rational?

> It is not within the power of this Court to correct flaws in the policies so long as they are supported by a rational basis.
> —*Cook v. Pamela Stewart*[1]

In 1972, the United States Supreme Court decided *San Antonio v. Rodriguez*, a seminal case in public school finance.[2] In *San Antonio,* the Court assessed the constitutionality of Texas's state school finance formula. Lawyers challenging the system argued that the U.S. Constitution guaranteed every child a fundamental right to an education and that Texas abridged that right. The thrust of their argument: the state's system, heavily reliant on local property taxes, disadvantaged property-poor school districts. The system, in effect, created two classes of school districts: the poor ones and wealthy ones.

Compelling facts supported the argument that two classes of school districts existed. Deep and wide resource disparities between property-poor and property-rich districts were documented. Even the state-defendants conceded that the school finance system had "imperfections" and "defects."[3] But the question before the court was not whether the finance system was simply *unequal* or *unfair*. The question was: did the school finance system create *unconstitutional inequalities*? The Supreme Court held that it did not.

How does *Rodriguez* relate to federal constitutional claims arising in VAM challenges? In brief, courts will apply a similar test (the rational basis test) and likely reach a similar result (upholding most evaluation laws based on VAMs). At least at the federal level, courts will tolerate an unfair law, so long as it is constitutional. Put another way, unwise policies and laws may, as a matter of law, be constitutional.[4] *Rodriguez* reminds us that challengers to VAMs have a high standard to satisfy if they are to persuade federal courts that current VAM laws are unconstitutional.

This chapter focuses on the constitutionality of VAMs. Specifically, to what extent, if any, do VAM-based evaluation systems violate a federal (or state) constitutional right?[5] To date, plaintiffs in states like Florida and Tennessee have argued that evaluation systems—and employment decisions based on these—violate portions of the Fourteenth Amendment to the U.S. Constitution.[6] They have not succeeded.

The chapter is organized as follows. It first discusses the applicable clauses of the Fourteenth Amendment (the equal protection and due process clauses) related to current challenges to VAMs in the courts. It then highlights two pre-VAM federal cases (*St. Louis Teachers' Union v. Board of Education of the City of St. Louis* and *Scheelhaase v. Woodbury Central Community School District*). Plaintiffs in both cases challenged adverse employment decisions that, in some way, involved student test scores. The cases have similar fact patterns to current and future VAM-based challenges.[7]

The chapter then focuses on the most recent (and telling) VAM cases in federal court. Two cases—*Cook v. Stewart*[8] and *Wagner v. Haslam*—receive considerable attention. Both are constitutional challenges to VAM evaluation systems. Teachers lost in both cases. These cases indicate that plaintiffs' chances of success in federal courts going forward are low.[9] To be sure, other theories of action that arise under state or contract law, as discussed in the next chapter, *may* be more successful. However, VAMs are constitutional under current federal case law.

THE FOUNDATIONS OF CONSTITUTIONAL CLAIMS: THE FOURTEENTH AMENDMENT

Before proceeding to a case law analysis, it is important to outline the federal constitutional claims available to plaintiffs. Specifically, three constitutional grounds form the basis of challenges to VAM-based evaluation systems and are derived from the Fourteenth Amendment. These are the:

1. Equal protection clause
2. Procedural due process clause
3. Substantive due process clause

The legal elements specific to each are discussed below. The case discussion that follows demonstrates how courts apply these clauses when considering challenges to VAMs.

THE EQUAL PROTECTION CLAUSE

The equal protection clause of the Fourteenth Amendment protects against government action that targets a particular group. It states as follows:

> No State shall make or enforce any law which shall . . . deny to any person within its jurisdiction the equal protection of the laws.[10]

This law prohibits state actors from treating different groups differently. If a law denies a benefit or right to a particular class of legally recognized *protected* citizens, a court will find it unconstitutional.

Court analysis of an equal protection claim is dictated by the nature of the groups impacted by the government law or action. Put another way, if the court determines a "special" group of people is impacted, it will closely scrutinize the law in question. First, the court determines if the challenged law covers a *protected* or *suspect* class. Protected classes include: race, religion, and national origin.

If a law treats members of protected or suspect classes differently, the court analyzes the challenged law under a *strict scrutiny standard*. The government must demonstrate a *compelling interest* in enacting the law and the means to meet that interest are *narrowly tailored*.[11] This is the government's burden to carry, and, importantly, strict scrutiny standard is a high (some might say impossible) bar for the government to satisfy.

If the class challenging the law is *not protected* (in essence, all those that have not been identified as protected), the court applies a *rational basis* review. This is a lower standard of review for the government to satisfy. It simply requires the government demonstrate a *legitimate interest* and that the means to meet that interest are *rationally related* to that interest. Typically, if a court analyzes a challenged law under rational basis, the law will be upheld.

An example of the levels of review may help clarify how they operate in context. Let's assume that a state passes a law (which all do) regulating the age that a person can receive a driver's license as seventeen (17). Assume further that a sixteen-year-old seeks to overturn the law in court because she feels that the age is too high. Her challenge would fail because, first, a court does not recognize youth as a protected class.[12] Second, the court would analyze her challenge (if brought under an equal protection clause) with a rational basis test. That low bar almost assures the government's success.

Let's return to the case of *San Antonio v. Rodriguez* to illustrate these concepts arising under the equal protection clause. The plaintiffs in *Rodriguez* urged the Court to recognize wealth as a *suspect* class of protected citizens. If it did so, the Court would have applied *strict scrutiny* review—a high standard for the government to meet—to assess the state's school finance system. However, the court declined to recognize wealth as a suspect class. It therefore applied the *rational basis test* to the Texas school finance system. Under this lower standard, the system may have been unfair, but it was constitutional.

PROCEDURAL DUE AND SUBSTANTIVE DUE PROCESS

Two other clauses of the Fourteenth Amendment have been used in actions challenging teacher evaluations. These are the procedural and substantive due process clauses. The applicable section of the Fourteenth Amendment where both of these clauses reside states as follows:

> No state shall make or enforce any law which shall abridge the privileges or immunities of citizens of the United States; *nor shall any state deprive any person of life, liberty, or property, without due process of law.* (emphasis supplied)[13]

Procedural Due Process

First, procedural due process is grounded in principles of fundamental fairness. It requires that the government adhere to certain processes when the *liberty or property rights* of a teacher are threatened, *before* that right is terminated.[14] In most instances involving teacher employment, a teacher's property right is implicated.[15] If a tenured teacher is facing dismissal, the government must adhere to certain processes to effectuate the termination. Procedural due process requires that a teacher receive notice of the proposed termination, an opportunity to challenge that decision, and a decision based on the facts.

In the context of VAMs, the procedural due process claim argument goes roughly as follows. A teacher challenging a termination decision contends that she did not receive sufficient notice to correct her performance issues. Specifically, because student test scores are typically released in the spring, a teacher can make the plausible argument that, by this point in the school year, the teacher does not have adequate time to alter instruction to rectify the situation and preserve her job for the following year. This seems patently unfair and, to the teacher, violates procedural due process.

Substantive Due Process

Substantive due process is triggered when the government impacts an individual's property right or interest. In the case of VAMs, governments—local school boards and legislatures—have adopted (by law or policy) numerous evaluation mechanisms using VAMs that could lead to a teacher losing her job. This is the property right at stake for teachers.

Courts, in assessing substantive due process claims, must first determine if the interest or right at stake is a *fundamental* right or not. Fundamental right is a legal term. Fundamental rights include the right to vote, and the right to marry, to name a few. Courts apply different standards of review with respect to the challenged law depending on this classification. If the interest is a *fundamental right*, the court will apply a *strict scrutiny* analysis. As discussed above, this is a high bar for the court to meet.

With respect to nonfundamental rights, courts apply a rational basis review. This is a low bar for the state-defendants (those seeking to uphold the law in question) to satisfy in their defense. To find that a state did not have a rational basis, the law would have to be arbitrary or capricious.[16] As a practical matter, if a law is reviewed under rational basis, it will survive.

PRE-VAM CASES INVOLVING TEACHER EVALUATIONS, EMPLOYMENT, AND STUDENT TEST SCORES

A line of pre-VAM cases exists regarding teacher challenges to evaluations. From an equal protection standpoint, courts have not found that teachers fall into a protected class (e.g., based on race or national origin they are treated differently). Similarly, from a due process perspective, courts applied the rational basis test, and found that the interests at hand do not implicate a *fundamental* right. Accordingly, courts typically applied the rational basis test.

Because courts frequently borrow from similar cases to decide new cases (e.g., cases involving VAMs), it is instructive to refer to these cases that are similar in many ways. Although they do not involve VAMs per se, they do involve challenges by teachers to evaluations and corresponding employment decisions that involved, in great part, reliance on student test scores.

St. Louis Teachers' Union v. Board of Education of the City of St. Louis

In 1987, a group of St. Louis teachers and their unions challenged the school district's use of student test scores on teachers' evaluations in *St. Louis Teachers' Union v. Board of Education of the City of St. Louis*.[17] The teachers filed claims under the Fourteenth Amendment's equal protection clause and its procedural and substantive process clauses.[18] The school district sought to dismiss the claims.

The teacher-plaintiffs argued that the district's use of the California Achievement Test (CAT) violated the *equal protection clause* because it created separate classes of teachers for purposes of ratings. The district used CAT scores only for teachers in English, communications, and mathematics; there was an irrational classification among different teacher groups, according to the teachers.

In addition, plaintiffs opposed the use of the preliminary ratings of teachers based on the CAT scores. Specifically, the district reviewed the overall evaluations (including other data) of only those teachers that received an "unsatisfactory" rating based on the CAT scores. In other words, the CAT scores became a gateway for the district to continue evaluation review (to substantiate the CAT score).

The court sided with the school district–defendant on the equal protection claims. The only question was whether the classification was *rationally related* to the district's objective to ensuring the competency of the district's teachers. Under this low bar of scrutiny, the court found it was. It commented that use of test scores for evaluation related to the district's overall objective of ensuring teacher competency.[19] Likewise, the use of the "unsatisfactory review" to seek further documentation indicating an unsatisfactory rating was not arbitrary or capricious.[20]

The teachers achieved some measure of victory in *St. Louis*. The court found that the teachers did have a property interest in "salary advancement" which was implicated by their negative evaluations. In other words, if the administration chose to withhold a bonus or salary incentive based on their evaluations, teachers were entitled to due process. Likewise, the court found that the teachers had a constitutional right to be free from "arbitrary and capricious actions" through the evaluation process that jeopardized their teaching positions.

However, it is important to note that the court only recognized that the plaintiffs had procedural and substantive due process rights. The *St. Louis* court did not hold that the use of the evaluation, as applied to the teachers, in fact, violated these rights.[21] Thus, *St. Louis* was something of a hollow victory for teachers.

Scheelhaase v. Woodbury Central Community School District

The case of *Scheelhaase v. Woodbury Central Community School District* provides some insight about court treatment of teacher evaluations regarding student progress on standardized tests.[22] At issue in *Scheelhaase* was the district's decision to use standardized test scores to rate a teacher and, ultimately, not renew her contract. In this case, much like other VAM cases today, the district relied almost primarily on the teacher's test scores to make their employment decision.

The teacher argued that the sole use of test scores as the grounds for her discharge "finds no support in educational policy."[23] Moreover, she made arguments relative to the interpretation of the tests. She asserted that the district erred in their interpretation of the tests. Under her review of the data, the tests demonstrated her students had made "normal progress." Thus, even assuming the use of test scores was a sound way to make an employment decision, the district failed to properly understand the data.

The court rejected the teacher's claims. The court's reasoning is significant. Simply put, the court concluded it did not have the jurisdiction to interfere with internal administrative decisions of local school officials. The court wrote:

> It is our holding that the administration of the internal affairs of the school district before us has not passed by judicial fiat from the local board, where it is lodged by statute, to the Federal court. Such matters as the competence of teachers, and the standards of its measurement are not, without more, matters of constitutional dimensions.[24]

Thus, the *Scheelhaase* decision expresses a court preference to defer to local school administrative decisions.

How do *St. Louis Teachers* and *Scheelhaase* relate to the current constitutional challenges to VAMs in federal court? There are parallels. First, the plaintiffs in *St. Louis Teachers* and *Scheelhaase* argued that overreliance on standardized test data reflected misguided policy. Put another way, the plaintiff-teachers attacked the evaluation system itself.

But, significantly, the *St. Louis Teachers* and *Scheelhaase* courts avoided the plaintiffs' invitation to debate the merits of the underlying policy. In fact, the *Scheelhaase* court was quite explicit in this point. In this vein, they reflect the sentiment expressed in the *San Antonio v. Rodriguez* case where that court acknowledged an unfair, but constitutional, choice of policy.

Second, both cases have precedential value. Courts that hear VAM cases will have to address one of the central issues in both *St. Louis Teachers* and *Scheelhaase*: to what extent does a court have the authority to overturn policy decisions made by school districts involving test data and teacher evaluation? *St. Louis Teachers* and *Scheelhaase* remain "good law." Thus, the *St. Louis Teachers* and *Scheelhaase* decisions will offer guidance for courts as they entertain similar questions that involve the use of VAMs.

Third, and in a sign of optimism for teacher-plaintiffs, the *St. Louis Teachers* court did find that teachers had a substantive due process claim regarding the use of evaluations that may impact their salary advancement. Current challenges to VAM-based evaluation policies have argued along a similar line—that where VAM-based evaluations impact bonuses, or merit pay, teachers have a constitutionally protected property interest.

Yet, importantly, this does not ensure a court agreement with the teachers' position that the system is unconstitutional. Rather, it only recognizes that there is a legal claim under the due process clause. In fact, *St. Louis Teachers* and *Scheelhaase* suggest that teacher claims will be defeated. Yet, because of this, educators do have an important tool—*a threat of litigation.* The significance of this is discussed in chapter 7.

CURRENT FEDERAL CONSTITUTIONAL CASES INVOLVING VAMs

Decided VAM Cases: *Cook v. Stewart* and *Wagner v. Haslam*

Two cases at the federal level warrant discussion because both represent direct challenges to VAM-based decisions. These cases are: *Wagner v. Haslam* and *Cook v. Stewart*. Both cases involve equal protection and substantive due process claims. A federal district court in Tennessee issued *Wagner*. The Eleventh Circuit Court of Appeals—a court sitting at the highest appellate level of the court system besides the Supreme Court—issued *Cook*. The *Cook* case is persuasive (but not binding) on courts outside of the Eleventh Circuit.[25] In both cases, the evaluations and employment decisions were upheld.

Wagner v. Haslam

Wagner involved a challenge to state and district policies for teacher evaluation in Tennessee. The policies had been enacted pursuant to Tennessee's "First to the Top Act." The act, passed in 2010 by the Tennessee legislature, required that teachers be evaluated, in part, on a value-added modeling assessment—TVAAS (Tennessee Value-Added Assessment

System).[26] The TVAAS collected data relative to only those subjects that were tested by TCAP (the Tennessee Comprehensive Assessment Program). TCAP was issued in subjects of mathematics, reading/language arts, social studies, and science in grades 3–8. Teachers in non-TCAP subjects were evaluated on school value-added results.[27]

Relevant facts from *Wagner* are as follows: Two teachers brought claims in federal court. Plaintiff Wagner taught physical education for over two decades. The other teacher, Brauner, taught visual arts for six years. For two consecutive years, the plaintiffs received bonuses based on the schoolwide TVAAS results. However, in the school year of 2013–2014, schoolwide TVAAS results declined. Therefore, the district denied Wagner and Brauner bonuses. In addition, Brauner was denied tenure.[28]

The plaintiffs claimed the state actions violated the substantive due process and equal protection clauses of the Fourteenth Amendment. Specifically, they argued that it was:

> arbitrary, capricious, and irrational to require that teachers be evaluated substantially on the basis of student standardized test scores unrelated to the courses they teach . . . [and] there is no rational reason to assign individual TVAAS scores to teachers of tested subjects while assigning school-wide TVAAS scores to teachers of non-tested subjects.[29]

The *Wagner* court dismissed the teachers' claims.

The court found a rational basis to the government's actions. Lawmakers *could believe* that a teacher impacts student performance on assessments in subject areas not in their instructional jurisdiction.[30] Moreover, a system could incentivize teachers to assist students in the TCAP subjects through supplemental tutoring. In addition, teachers may be inclined to integrate TCAP subjects into instruction of the non-TCAP subjects. Taken together, the evaluation laws were grounded in a rational basis.[31]

By way of contrast, the plaintiffs could not demonstrate the system was irrational or arbitrary. Indeed, the court noted some extreme examples that *could* demonstrate irrationality. For instance, if the system based a Tennessee teacher's evaluation on test results from Arizona students, the regimen would be irrational. In another example, the court indicated that if an evaluation was based on a baseball team's record, that too would be irrational. These examples are certainly outliers, but reflect how difficult it is for plaintiffs to win in cases where a rational review is applied.

To be sure, the court did sympathize with the teachers regarding the system's unfairness. But, under the rational basis test, policymakers are allowed, according to the court, to make both "excellent" and "terrible" decisions.[32] So long as there is some *conceivable* "modicum of rationality" the court cannot disturb the decision.[33]

Cook v. Stewart

Cook v. Stewart is a significant case in VAM litigation. It represents a question of first impression at the appellate level of the federal court system: whether VAM-based evaluations and employment decisions are constitutional under the equal protection and due process clauses of the U.S. Constitution. In 2014, a trial court ruled that they were. In 2015, the federal circuit court of appeals agreed and upheld the state's evaluation system.

Significantly, *Cook* binds all the states in the Eleventh Circuit and it is persuasive authority in all other courts of appeals. Thus, other federal courts addressing the issue will have to adopt or distinguish the logic in *Cook*. Both decisions—from the district court and appeals court—are discussed below. The trial court discussion sets forth the important facts which remain unchanged in the analysis of the appellate court.

Cook v. Stewart: The District Court (trial court) Decision

The facts of *Cook* are as follows.[34] The challenged evaluation system required teacher evaluations and employment decisions to be determined, in great part, with reference to "student learning growth."[35] It also required the use of the state's standardized assessments (the FCAT) for this purpose and, in turn, these results were required to be used in employment decisions.[36] The FCAT tested students in reading and math for grades 4–8. Thus, some teachers did not instruct students in the FCAT areas (e.g., music teachers).

The evaluation system created three (3) tiers of teachers. Type A teachers were those assessed directly by VAMs applicable to the subject areas in which they taught (e.g., those subjects under the FCAT). Type B teachers consisted of those where the FCAT was used as a proxy for student growth measures of students that they taught, but not in the FCAT subjects. For example, a seventh grade reading assessment of students could be used as part of a seventh grade science teacher's VAM rating, assuming the science teacher taught those students for purposes of science.

Type C teachers were those teachers who did not "share" students who were subject to the FCAT. In this instance, superintendents could establish "instructional teams." The student measure of growth component of a teacher's evaluation could then be based on growth of the "instructional teams' students' growth on statewide assessments." Significantly, the term "instructional team" was not defined.

Substantive Due Process Challenge

Type B and Type C teachers challenged the state and district evaluation policies on due process grounds arguing that the tiered system was irrational. In effect, the teachers contended that it was arbitrary and irrational to evaluate teachers based on tests for subjects they did not teach.

The court applied the deferential rational basis test because no fundamental interest was implicated. Thus, the question before the court was whether the state had a legitimate interest to develop the evaluation system and, if it did, were the means rational (or not arbitrary) to pursue this interest? With respect to the first question, the court concluded that the government had a legitimate interest—an increase in student learning growth.

The court then assessed whether the means to achieve that interest was rational for both B and C teachers. With respect to Type B teachers, the court noted that it was rational to "consider the students' improvement" when evaluating teachers, notwithstanding that improvement occurred outside of that teacher's instructional domain.[37]

The court then applied a similar analysis to Type C teachers (those who did not have any instructional contact with students). The court here again found a rational basis and wrote:

> [P]rofessional teachers could positively impact *all* student at their schools by fostering an encouraging learning environment, influencing and inspiring other teachers, exhibiting leadership, participating in

school-wide strategic efforts, or otherwise making efforts to improve overall student learning.[38]

In addition, the court found that there was a rational belief that these collective efforts might "incentivize better teaching," thereby advancing the state's interest in increasing student growth.[39]

Equal Protection Claims

The court also assessed the teachers' equal protection argument and found in favor of the government. Here the teachers argued that the evaluation policies created separate classes of teachers (e.g., Types A, B, and C) and, in doing, so, violated this clause of the Fourteenth Amendment.[40] It is worth remembering that, so long as a class is not suspect or protected, the court must apply a rational review to the challenged law.

Because the classes at issue in *Cook* were not "protected" (e.g., classes established by race or national origin) a rational basis review applied. Similar to the analysis of the due process claims, the court noted that there is a legitimate government interest in evaluating teachers based on "the student growth learning measures that are *available* to the districts."[41]

Importantly, the district court judge distinguished between an unfair evaluation law and an *unconstitutional* one. The court did characterize the system as "unfair." That the unfair evaluation system was tightly connected to employment decisions was also concerning. He wrote:

> To make matters worse, the legislature has mandated that teacher ratings be used to make important employment decisions such as pay, promotion, assignment, and retention. Ratings affect a teacher's professional reputation as well because they are made public—they have even have been printed in the newspaper. Needless to say, this Court would be hard-pressed to find anyone who would find this evaluation system fair to non-FCAT teachers, let alone be willing to submit to a similar evaluation system.[42]

But an "unfair" evaluation system is distinguishable from an *unconstitutional* one. And here is where the plaintiffs' case failed.

The court concluded with the following:

> This case is not about the fairness of the evaluation system. *The standard of review is not whether the evaluation policies are good or bad, wise or unwise, but whether the evaluation policies are rational within the meaning of the law.*[43]

The plaintiffs exposed an unfair and unsound evaluation system. But it was still constitutional.

Cook v. Stewart: The Eleventh Circuit Court of Appeals Decision

The plaintiffs appealed the district court ruling to the Eleventh Circuit Court of Appeals.[44] The court of appeals affirmed the district court's decision. The appeals court adopted district court's reasoning and wrote:

> [The defendants] argue that the policies are rationally related to the purpose behind the *Student Success Act* itself which is to "increase student academic performance by improving the quality of instructional, administrative, and supervisory services in the public schools of the state.[45]

The *Cook* appellate decision is significant. First, the decision binds federal courts in all states in the Eleventh Circuit (Georgia and Alabama). To the extent that these states have (or wish to adopt) similar VAM-based evaluation systems, they will not find any federal constitutional barriers. *Cook* effectively forecloses constitutional challenges to VAM evaluation and employment decisions in these states.

Second, the case is *persuasive* authority for all other federal jurisdictions. Courts in other appellate jurisdictions must consider the *Cook* result, although they are not required to adopt it.[46] The persuasive power of *Cook* was demonstrated in *Wagner v. Haslam,* discussed above. The *Wagner* court, in dismissing the Tennessee teachers' constitutional claim, cited *Cook* (at that time, the *Cook* case was not at the appellate level). Courts in other jurisdictions cannot ignore *Cook* if and when they face similar decisions. They are not required to adopt its logic, but, at minimum, they will have to address it.

OTHER CASES AT THE FEDERAL COURT LEVEL

Trout v. Knox County Board of Education and Taylor v. Haslam

Two cases—consolidated into one—are currently pending in federal district court in Tennessee. The teacher-plaintiffs in the cases of *Trout v. Knox County Board of Education* and *Taylor v. Haslam* are challenging the use of individualized test scores in employment decisions.

In brief, the facts of the case are as follows. The teacher in *Trout* taught Algebra II in an alternative school for the school years of 2010–2011 and 2011–2012. Her evaluation score for the 2011–2012 year was among the highest possible. Based on this, she assumed that she would receive a bonus. However, because of a clerical error, her scores were misreported and she did not receive the bonus. The teacher in *Taylor* taught eighth grade physical science. Only twenty-two of 143 of his students took the eighth grade TVAAS science test and, based on these scores, he received the lowest possible rating. He was denied a bonus.

The plaintiffs in *Trout* and *Taylor* raise several arguments. They contend that the TVAAS estimates are an arbitrary measure of student performance. They have also attacked the system based on the limited subset of students used to calculate their rating. In both *Trout* and *Taylor* only one class taught by each teacher, respectively, was used to create the relevant evaluations. This limited course selection, they argue, does not adequately represent their teaching ability.

Both *Trout* and *Taylor*, as of this writing, are pending. Yet, importantly, the plaintiffs in each will have to reconcile their claims with the *Wagner* and *Cook* decisions. While the *Cook* and *Wagner* decisions concerned challenges to ratings based on scores for students that they did not teach, the decisions embrace a consistent theme; the choice of evaluation mechanisms may be statistically flawed and unfair, but it is not the courts' responsibility to overrule the legislature's choice of action. Thus, it is likely that *Trout* and *Wagner* will not be successful, at least with respect to their federal constitutional claims.

Houston Federation of Teachers v. Houston Independent School District

Another case—*Houston Federation of Teachers v. Houston Independent School District*—is also winding its way through federal court. In *Houston* the plaintiffs have argued that the evaluation systems have incentivized administrators to misuse VAM scores. In particular, the plaintiff-teachers allege that district-level administrators pressured principals to align in-class observations to comport with the low VAM-scores.[47] Moreover, the plaintiffs in *Houston* have alleged that the district has not provided important underlying information regarding the VAMs, such as the methodological assumptions behind the chosen VAM.[48]

The *Houston* case raises an additional layer that distinguishes it from the other cases discussed here. In *Houston* the chief complaint is that administrators are intentionally misapplying the evaluation system. If such allegations prove to be factually accurate, it would bolster the claim that administrators are acting with caprice and, therefore, it would not survive rational scrutiny review.[49]

The *Houston* case has not yet been heard. The allegations are just that—allegations that require some level of proof. However, the case represents another tactic and legal theories used to challenge VAMs as they are applied.[50] It is likely that, as federal claims are foreclosed, other theories will emerge.

STATE LAW CONSTITUTIONAL CLAIMS

In addition, VAMs and their attending employment decisions can be challenged under state law. Indeed, possible rights of action may arise under the following: state constitution, teacher tenure statutes, state labor laws governing public employee relationships, collective bargaining agreements, and breach of contract. These legal frameworks are discussed briefly below along with relevant cases that are just emerging.

State constitutions generally provide for procedural and substantive due process protections. Accordingly, teachers may seek a claim of relief under their respective state constitutions. This line of claim may be may be particularly advantageous, depending on particular state statute or constitutions. Challenges to state laws, such as those related to school finance claims, have had better success under state law rather than federal law.[51]

A state law claim is currently pending in New Mexico in the case of *Stewart v. New Mexico Public Education Department.*[52] Here, the teacher-plaintiffs and their union stated that the VAM-based evaluation policies adopted by the state Department of Education violate the following provisions of the state constitution.[53] The case is significant because it may be a bellwether of other claims based on state constitutional provisions.

The New York Cases: *Ahern v. King* and *Urbanski v. King*

In New York State, teachers' unions have brought two separate actions, *Ahern v. King* and *Urbanski v. King.*[54] Both actions contend that the evaluation systems violate that state's constitution. Teachers and unions in Syracuse (the *Ahern* case) and Rochester (the *Urbanski* case), respectively, argued that the state's evaluation system violated the equal protection clause of the constitution. Both contend that the evaluation system does not properly account for the effects of *poverty* on teachers' ratings.[55] Because of this omission, the evaluation system is irrational, arbitrary, and capricious. The cases are pending in New York state trial courts.

It is unclear whether state constitutional claims represent more friendly venues for plaintiffs challenging evaluation laws and regulations. While the federal constitution is silent on any right to education, all states have a specific constitutional education clause. Because of this, plaintiffs have enjoyed considerable success in school finance claims litigated under state constitutions.

Some advocates succeeded advancing particular policy reforms through litigation under state education clauses. This was evident in *Vergara v. California.* In *Vergara,* plaintiffs successfully attacked that state's tenure statutes at the trial level on the grounds that the statutes deprived students of their state education rights. The case is on appeal.

In addition, school finance cases have successfully used state education clauses in this regard. In *Rose v. Council for Better Education,*[56] the Kentucky Supreme Court struck down as unconstitutional the state's entire school finance system. That contrasts with *San Antonio v. Rodriguez,* where the U.S. Supreme Court upheld the Texas state school finance system. Yet, as many have noted, courts may be reluctant to engage the constitution with what they perceive as inherently political (and, therefore, policy) questions. Thus, it is likely that the state constitutional challenges to VAM-based evaluation systems face an uphill climb.

KEY POINTS

- Challenges to VAM-based evaluations are just now developing in the court system, but there are several cases worth noting.
- Prior to the advent of VAMs, federal courts have heard constitutional challenges to teacher evaluations that use student test scores. In those cases, discussed here, the courts have found the design and application of those systems constitutional.
- The question concerning the constitutionality of VAM-based evaluation systems has reached the federal appellate level. Specifically, the Eleventh Circuit Court of Appeals has addressed the matter in the case of *Cook v. Stewart*. The *Cook* court found that Florida's evaluation system was constitutional under a rational basis review.
- However, federal courts have noted that the evaluations systems, while constitutional, may be unwise as a matter of policy.
- Other claims are emerging with respect to challenges to VAMs based on state law. In particular, state constitutions may provide a possible legal theory of action.
- The discussion concerning U.S. constitutional challenges provides a useful lesson for those seeking a court remedy to VAMs. Indeed, early signs suggest that federal courts are unwilling to overturn a state legislature's choice of evaluation.
- Importantly, the *threat of litigation* remains. Even though plaintiffs' chances of victory in the federal (and perhaps state) courts may be dwindling, lawsuits can draw attention to the absurd results that VAMs can require.

NOTES

1. *Cook v. Stewart*, 28 F. Supp. 3d 1207, 1214 (N.D. Fla., May 6, 2014), *6 (dismissing claims that the Florida teacher evaluation system is unconstitutional).

2. *San Antonio Independent School District v. Rodriguez,* 411 U.S. 1 (1973) (holding that there is no fundamental right to an education under the U.S. Constitution and wealth is not a protected class under the equal protection clause).

3. Ibid. at 17.

4. Ibid. at 4.

5. The chapter focuses heavily on U.S. constitutional issues because the earliest litigation concerned federal claims. That said, there are state claims.

6. As noted in the state cases that follow, plaintiffs may raise arguments against VAMs arising under state constitutional provisions of a similar nature.

7. To be sure, it is recognized that VAMs and/or student growth measures are different in the sense that they are statistical models intended to better refine a link between a teacher and student progress. Yet, at bottom, the use of standardized tests for evaluation and then employment decisions is the underlying theme present.

8. *Cook v. Stewart* (district court holding), supra, note 1; *Cook v. Bennett,* 792 F. 3d 1294 (11th Cir. 2015) (appeals court decision affirming, in full, lower court opinion in *Cook v. Stewart*).

9. The *Cook v. Bennett* ruling deserves considerable attention because it reached the highest appellate level of the federal court system, with the exception of the Supreme Court. Thus, *Cook* has significant precedential value.

10. U.S. Constitution, amendment XIV, section 1.

11. See, for example, *City of Cleburne v. Cleburne Living Ctr.*, 473 U.S. 432, 440–441 (discussing the application of various levels of scrutiny courts will apply to assess constitutionality of state law or regulation).

12. To be sure, age is a protected class under certain federal employment statutes (e.g., the Age Discrimination in Employment Act of 1967). However, to qualify in this protected class, the age would have to be above forty (40) years old. In addition, some cases have recognized that children could be a "quasi-suspect" class, allowing a court to analyze a challenge at a higher level of scrutiny than rational basis. See, for example, *Plyler v. Doe,* 457 U.S. 202 (1982).

13. Ibid., *Plyler v. Doe* at 244.

14. See, for example, *Perry v. Sindermann,* 408 U.S. 593 (1972).

15. However, the *liberty* right of teachers to pursue employment and their interest in keeping a good reputation may become an issue, especially as districts and states seek to publicly report teacher evaluation ratings. For instance, teachers labeled "ineffective" may find that the rating damages their reputation such that it prevents them from gaining employment.

16. See, for example, *Cook v. Stewart,* supra, note 8. In this case, the Eleventh Circuit Court of Appeals upheld Florida's evaluation law under a rational basis test.

17. *St. Louis Teachers' Union Local 420 v. Board of Education of City of St. Louis*, 652 F. Supp. 425 (E.D.: Mo. 1987).
18. Ibid.
19. Ibid.
20. Ibid. at 431.
21. Ibid. at 435–436.
22. *Scheelhaase v. Woodbury Central Community School District*, 488 F.2d 237 (8th Cir. 1973).
23. Ibid. at 239.
24. Ibid. at 243–244. The point that the management of personnel is strictly under the purview of school officials is explored in greater detail in the next chapter.
25. Put another way, courts in other jurisdictions must refer to the case. However, they do not have to follow the case and may distinguish it based on the particular facts of that case.
26. *Wagner v. Haslam*, 2015 WL 3658165 (M.D. Tenn. 2015), *2.
27. See *Board Policy* 5.201 Tennessee State Board of Education (April 19, 2013).
28. *Wagner v. Haslam*, note 26, at *2.
29. Ibid. at *12.
30. Ibid. at *16.
31. Ibid.
32. Ibid. at *15.
33. Ibid.
34. *Cook v. Stewart*, 28 F. Supp. 3d 1207 (N.D. Fla. 2014).
35. Ibid. at 1209.
36. Ibid. at 1215–1216.
37. Ibid. at 1213.
38. Ibid.
39. Ibid.
40. Recall that courts apply different levels of scrutiny depending on the group of people affected by the state action. Laws that implicate "protected classes" (those that are based on race, origin) receive strict scrutiny. A challenged law impacting nonprotected classes would be examined under the deferential rational basis test.
41. *Cook v. Stewart*, supra, note 1, at 1214.
42. Ibid. at 1215–1216.
43. Ibid. at 1216.
44. The defendants named in the case changed. However, the Eleventh Circuit's July 7, 2015, opinion was its decision in the appeal of the *Cook v. Stewart* decision. *Cook v. Bennett*, supra, note 8.

45. *Cook v. Bennett* at 1301.

46. In total, there are thirteen (13) appellate level courts. For an overview of the federal court system, see www.uscourts.gov/about-federal-courts/court-role-and-structure/comparing-federal-state-courts, accessed January 25, 2016.

47. Plaintiffs' Original Complaint, *Houston Federation of Teachers v. Houston Independent School District*, Case No. 4:14-cv-01189 (S.D. Tex., April 30, 2014), 22. The district contracts with an entity that generates the VAM scores.

48. Ibid. It noted that in a survey conducted by the teachers union, 74 percent of district administrators felt "pressured" to give lower scores on observations.

49. The misuse of student test—toward illegal and unethical ends—has emerged as a growing trend in education.

50. Federal trial courts in Tennessee are currently considering two other cases related to constitutional claims. At the moment, like the case in *Houston,* the court has not issued a decision. For reference, these cases are: *Trout v. Knox County Board of Education*, Case No. 3:14-cv-49 (E.D. Tenn.), and *Taylor v. Haslam,* Case No. 3:14-cv-113 (M.D. Tenn.).

51. For example, the U.S. Supreme Court in *San Antonio v. Rodriguez* effectively foreclosed challenges to state school finance systems arising under the U.S. Constitution. Yet, in response, plaintiffs sought relief under state constitutions and, by most accounts, have been successful. See, for example, *Rose v. Council for Better Education, Inc., 790 S.W.2d 186 (1989).*

52. *State of New Mexico, ex rel., Stewart, et al. v. New Mexico Public Education Department,* Complaint for Declaratory and Preliminary and Permanent Injunctive Relief, July 2, 2015, accessed April 4, 2016, www.aft.org/sites/default/files/nm-complaint-teacherevals_1114.pdf.

53. Ibid.

54. Petitioner's Memorandum of Law, *Ahern v. King* (N.Y. Sup. Ct., April 14, 2014), and NYSUT Media Relations, "Suit: State failed to account for impact of poverty in evaluations," March 10, 2014, accessed April 4, 2015, www.nysut.org/news/2014/March/suit-state-failed-to-account-for-impact-of-poverty-in-evaluations.

55. In New York, like other states, the evaluation of teachers requires the use of student growth measures.

56. 790 S.W.2d 186, 60 Ed. Law Rep. 1289 (1989)

4

PRE-EXISTING CONDITIONS

Legal Deference to School Administrators' Judgment of Teacher Performance

> The problem for them [the School Board] and this court, however, is that the statute requiring primary reliance on the FCAT and similar tests leaves no room for the free-form exercise of professional expertise they advocate.
> —*Sherrod v. Palm Beach County School Board*[1]

In theory, VAMs should ease both the process of dismissing a teacher and the defense of that decision, if needed. Because VAMs purportedly link student performance to a particular teacher, underperforming teachers can be easily identified. If a teacher fails to improve, the case for dismissal is strengthened. In this way, VAMs seemingly provide irrefutable grounds for termination. If challenged, a VAM-based evaluation system—which, at its core, is based on standardized test scores[2]—will prove compelling to a third party, like a court. At least that's the theory.

These assumptions are facile. First, *VAMs are entirely unnecessary* to defend an adverse employment decision. Because most state statutes and court decisions—at least those that predate VAMs—already vest local school officials with the authority to make and defend a decision, the addition of a VAM requirement is duplicative. Moreover, courts like to hear—and will defer to—administrators' reasoned perspectives regarding teacher performance.

Second, and more concerning, *VAMs actually complicate* a district's case, if challenged. Because of the statistical concerns regarding validity of VAMs, they create an opportunity for teachers to attack the underlying merits of a termination or other adverse employment decision. Their conflicting and confusing nature is fodder for a plaintiff's lawyer. At the same time, VAMs restrict a court from deferring to school administrators' judgment regarding performance. Cases in Florida, especially at the administrative level, illustrate the complicating nature of VAMs in performance-based terminations, and receive much attention in this chapter.[3]

At bottom, this chapter questions the wisdom of legally requiring VAMs for evaluation and employment matters. If the law already defers to the subjective opinions of administrators when they make employment decisions, why introduce a questionable metric of teacher performance like VAMs? Why create more risk (at the very least, added complications for school districts' cases) by *legally requiring* the use of VAMs through statutes at the expense of school administrators' judgment?

The chapter first traces the legal underpinnings of local control over personnel and establishes the simple point that administrators had all the necessary tools to successfully defend high-stakes employment decisions. Specifically, state law under constitutions, statutes, and regulations generally defers to the school administrators' reasoned professional judgment regarding significant personnel decisions.

Yet the chapter then notes that legal mandates of VAMs dilute this deference, requiring courts to essentially veto school administrators' opinions regarding performance. Accordingly, this complicates a district's case to terminate underperforming teachers. This has happened in Florida and cases there are discussed in this chapter.

ORIGINS OF SCHOOL DISTRICT AUTHORITY REGARDING PERSONNEL DECISIONS

State Constitutions: The Origins of Public School Systems and Local Control

State constitutions provide the legal foundation for public schools and serve as the starting point for understanding local control over school personnel. They require state legislatures to establish a system of public schools. For example, Wisconsin's constitution reads as follows:

> [T]he legislature shall provide by law for the establishment of district schools, which shall be as nearly uniform as practicable.[4]

Other state constitutions employ similar language.[5] Toward fulfilling this duty, state legislatures create school finance systems, and state departments of education regulate the operation of schools.

In addition, the legislature delegates day-to-day management to local school officials. This includes the authority to manage personnel matters. Most states provide that school superintendents and boards control hiring of teachers.[6] A demonstrative example from New Hampshire reads:

> Superintendents shall nominate and school boards shall elect all teachers in their school administrative unit, providing that such teachers hold [applicable credentials].[7]

Other states have adopted a similar two-step process.[8]

Statutes also provide local officials with the authority to terminate teachers. In Florida, for example, the superintendent and school board have discretion over dismissal decisions.[9] This may seem elementary, but the point cannot be understated: local school officials have the authority to staff their schools as they see fit. Until recently, states' legislatures have ensured that the power to evaluate and direct personnel resides with school officials.

To be certain, this power is not unfettered. Administrators cannot violate state statutes, constitution, or federal laws (e.g., those prohibiting discrimination based on race or gender).[10] In addition, tenure statutes require certain procedural protections against arbitrary termination decisions. Tenure provides *due process*; before a teacher is terminated, they receive *notice* and a *hearing* of the proposed action. Moreover, tenure statutes specify grounds for termination (e.g., incompetence, etc.).[11] Tenure is not "lifetime employment," contrary to popular opinion.

A Connecticut statute (in effect pre-VAM)[12] governing continuing contract or tenured employees illustrates the concepts of due process and tenure. In that state, a teacher must be notified that the district intends to terminate employment.[13] A tenured teacher contract can be terminated on the following grounds: (1) inefficiency, incompetence or ineffectiveness;

(2) insubordination against reasonable rules of the board of education; (3) moral misconduct; (4) disability, as shown by competent medical evidence; (5) elimination of the position; (6) other due and sufficient cause.[14] The school board holds a hearing on the recommendation.[15]

A teacher can appeal a school board decision. However, as Connecticut illustrates, courts prefer to affirm the school board's judgment.[16] Thus, contrary to popular belief,[17] tenure does not prohibit administrators from exercising their discretion with respect to terminating underperforming teachers.[18]

State Court Case Law Demonstrating Court Deference to School District Personnel Decisions

Courts consistently defer to school administrators' decisions regarding high-stakes employment decisions. Moreover, courts emphasize administrators' input over "objective" measures, such as test scores, when reaching their decision. Prior to the advent of VAMs, court decisions reflect limited, if any, reliance, on test scores to uphold a district's decision regarding employment status. To be sure, courts consider student growth and test performance. But courts view test scores in light of the whole evidentiary picture. They are not dispositive and, in the past, not an evidentiary requirement.

Several caveats are in order before discussing the cases that illustrate these concepts. The cases presented immediately below—*Whaley v. Anoka* and *Johnson v. Francis Howell*—predate VAMs. Moreover, they are illustrative, not exhaustive. Yet, importantly, the cases do present consistent themes: (1) courts value of the opinions of school administrators in assessing teacher performance above all else; and (2) test scores provide little, if any value, to the final decision of a court in upholding a district's decision.

Pre-VAM Cases Involving Test Scores, Teacher Performance, and Deference to Administrators

Whaley v. Anoka

The case of *Whaley v. Anoka-Hennepin Independent School District*[19] illustrates the significance of school administrators' opinions in contested termination cases relative to the value of test scores in upholding a personnel decision; it also is important because it demonstrates how courts treat student test scores from an evidentiary perspective.

The facts of *Whaley* are as follows. In February of 1981, the Anoka-Hennepin school board (the "district") terminated Gerald Whaley. Mr. Whaley was a tenured teacher. He had served as a principal in the district. During the year he was terminated, Mr. Whaley taught reading in grades four, five, and six.

Prior to his dismissal, the district notified Mr. Whaley regarding his deficient performance. In May of 1980, the district gave Whaley a notice of deficiency in the following areas:

1. Poor rapport with students;
2. Insufficient communication with parents and fellow staff members;
3. Inappropriate use of class time;
4. Failure to be punctual or appear at appointments;
5. Failure to follow the school board's adopted reading program;
6. Irrational grading of students; and
7. Lack of student progress.

The district warned Whaley that if he did not improve in these areas, they would terminate his contract.

The district closely monitored Whaley's instruction. School administrators observed and evaluated his instruction on six (6) separate occasions between the beginning of the school year in 1980 (September) and January 1981. Mr. Whaley participated in meetings to discuss his teaching. Ultimately, the district did not see improvement and moved to terminate Whaley.

Whaley challenged the dismissal and the case ultimately reached the Minnesota Supreme Court. The state supreme court upheld the district's decision. The court indicated that the identified deficiencies noted by the district (e.g., excessive use of worksheets, lack of student discipline, lack of student progress) were supported by "substantial evidence."

What types of evidence constituted "substantial evidence"? The court's finding relied, in great part, on the testimony of the opinions of administrators based on observations of Whaley's teaching. For example, the court opined:

> [T]he school principal, who observed Whaley's use of worksheets and assessed the effect of such use on students, testified that Whaley used worksheets to such an extent that it frustrated students and *inhibited their progress*.[20]

The principal's judgment—which is evidenced in the form of testimony—substantiated, in great part, the final conclusion that Whaley should be terminated.

The court considered student tests scores, to a limited degree. It noted Whaley's poor performance was evident, in part, by lack of student achievement on tests, which supported a conclusion regarding Whaley's performance. Yet, significantly, the court relied on the opinions of school officials to support this point. The court stated that a school reading specialist and another teacher compared Whaley's students' scores to those of other students and concluded they had "progressed more slowly than other students in the program."[21] The court was satisfied with this level of analysis with respect to the test progress. It did not need more (e.g., a VAM-like complicated statistical analysis).

Johnson v. Francis Howell R-3 Board of Education[22]

The case of *Johnson v. Howell R-3 Board of Education* reaffirms the value of the opinions of school administrators as evidence *over* test scores, at least in the wisdom of court decisions. *Johnson* was brought in Missouri state court and involved the dismissal of a tenured teacher. In *Johnson* the district sought to remove a tenured teacher on the grounds that she was "incompetent" and "inefficient."[23]

The basic facts in *Johnson* follow. The teacher, Barbara Johnson, began her teaching career in 1974 as an elementary teacher. Concerns about her teaching arose between 1983 and 1985. Administrators noted she had difficulty "individualizing instruction, creating a positive learning environment . . . and establishing positive relationships with her students."[24] The district requested that Ms. Johnson observe other teachers and attend professional development workshops. Ms. Johnson complied.

Ms. Johnson improved but concerns remained. Therefore, the district placed her on a professional development plan in 1991. Despite completing the plan, the school administration concluded deficiencies persisted, especially in the area of classroom management. Accordingly, in October of 1991, the superintendent notified the teacher by letter that she faced termination.

A few important facts are likely relevant to the court's ultimate decision and, importantly, reflect best practices for administrators. For example, school officials attempted to assist Ms. Johnson. They reviewed videos of her teaching and made comments for improvement. They issued seventeen memoranda on ways she could improve based on their thirty observations of her instruction. The teacher participated in role-playing exercises with administrators and teachers.

Notwithstanding these efforts, the teacher did not satisfy the expectations of school administrators. The school board held hearings and, ultimately, agreed with the administration's recommendation to terminate. They concluded that "although some improvement took place in her performance . . . her improvement was not sufficient to raise her performance to a satisfactory level."[25] Ms. Johnson, naturally, disagreed and sought a remedy in the courts.

Standardized test scores became a significant point of contention and a basis for Ms. Johnson's challenge to the district. Indeed, Ms. Johnson argued student test growth *supported* her position. Her students' scores improved, she noted. Therefore, her students had made progress in direct response to the intervention she had made regarding her teaching. Even school administrators admitted that she had made improvement.

Yet, notwithstanding her argument around test scores, the court affirmed her termination. In effect, the court diminished the test score evidence, allowing the administrators' opinion to carry the day. Here again, the flexibility afforded in the statute gives deference to evidence of administrators' testimony and their expert opinions. It allowed the court to take a wider view of the situation—to include other points of data that school administrators viewed as equally, if not more, important to the quality of her teaching.

In upholding the termination, the court downplayed the significance of student progress on tests. It wrote:

> *Even assuming* that the standardized test scores and appellant's testimony weigh in her favor, the principal's and assistant principal's evaluations, and the assistant principal's testimony, indicated that appellant still had teaching deficiencies. . . . Thus, the Board's decision was based on sufficient evidence, and we defer to the Board's decision, *even if* the evidence could support a different conclusion.[26]

The *Johnson* case is instructive. The teacher's use of the test scores foreshadows one argument that teachers under VAM evaluation systems may embrace: teachers may use them to undercut a school district's opinion of a teacher's performance formed through evaluations and opinions. The applicable evaluation and termination standards *did not require* the district to emphasize student growth on test scores. That flexibility defeated the teacher's most compelling arguments: that the standardized test scores of her students improved; that her methods had resulted in student progress.

Yet had the court been *required* to view those scores (and the student progress) by some statutory standard (as is the case in many states now because of VAMs), the district's case would have been weakened. Put another way: standardized test scores could have been used to *cut against the district's case* and, perhaps, might have led to a reversal of the school administrator's judgment. At the very least, the teacher's argument would have been strengthened.

Understanding *Whaley* and *Johnson* Together

Significant points emerge from *Whaley* and *Johnson*, in particular when we read the cases above together. Of note, courts place substantial evidentiary weight on school administrators' opinions regarding teacher performance. Cases in other jurisdictions substantiate this point.[27] Moreover, both courts were unencumbered by any specific requirements concerning test scores. Accordingly, the *Whaley* and *Johnson* courts (and others)[28] could rely primarily on administrators' judgment without mandated reference to student test scores.

A BREWING VAM STORM: FORESHADOWING IN FLORIDA

The requirement of VAMs in evaluation and employment matters complicates decisions and weakens school districts' cases if challenged, especially at the state court and administrative level. Examples in Florida illustrate this point. In these cases, presented below, the use of mandated VAMs allowed teachers an opportunity to exploit the statistical weaknesses in those models and, consequently, weaken the district's case.

To be sure, Florida recently amended some of its teacher evaluation requirements since the cases below were decided.[29] But those amendments are largely irrelevant to the primary conclusion presented here which is: evaluation statutes require focus and attention to student achievement on tests, and this forces courts to de-emphasize their deference to professional administrators' judgment in terms of evidentiary value and elevate test score performance.

The leading cases in Florida on this matter, *Sherrod v. Palm Beach County School Board* and *Young v. Palm Beach County School Board*, are discussed below. Together, they have influenced court and administrative review of challenges to terminations involving student achievement, especially as it relates to standardized tests, particularly in the *Sherrod* holding. The next section discusses numerous teacher termination cases in Florida that have applied *Sherrod* to defeat, or at least frustrate, school district claims of cause for termination of poor-performing teachers on the basis of student performance as assessed, in part, through standardized test scores.

Sherrod v. Palm Beach County School Board[30]

In the 2003–2004, the Palm Beach County School Board moved to discharge Curtis Sherrod.[31] The district documented numerous complaints about the teacher's abilities, including his presentation of subject matter, communication capacity, recordkeeping, capacity for working with others, and use of R-rated movies. He failed to follow lesson plans. Students did not have assigned readings for his classes. Based on this evidence it seemed clear that Mr. Sherrod was a poor quality teacher deserving termination.

Notwithstanding the well-documented observational records of Sherrod's poor performance, a court of appeals in Florida disagreed with the district's decision. Why? The court concluded that the district failed to follow mandated statutory guidelines governing evaluations. The applicable statutes required consideration of test scores, something the district failed to do. Without that evidence, the court concluded that it could not sustain the discharge.

Florida's state statute—which required *some* consideration of test scores—forced the court to overturn the district's decision. That statute read, in part:

> [T]he assessment procedure for instructional personnel . . . must be *primarily* based on the performance of students assigned to their classrooms.

Moreover, performance was to be primarily assessed by way of student performance on mandated tests. The applicable statute read that student performance:[32]

> must *primarily* use data and indicators of improvement in student performance assessed annually as specified [statute omitted] and may consider the results of peer reviews in evaluating the employee's performance.[33]

However, because the annual evaluations and the district's case did not incorporate this factor, *as required by statute,* the appellate court could not sustain the discharge.

Importantly, the statutory requirement minimized the value of the professional judgment of the administrators. The *Sherrod* court commented on this impact. It wrote:

> The problem for them [The School Board] and this court, however, is that the statute requiring primary reliance on the FCAT and similar tests leaves no room for the free-form exercise of professional expertise they advocate. [The statute] does not allow this kind of discretion even it is deemed superior by those with advanced evaluation skills.[34]

The court cautioned that the narrow focus on test scores could lead to absurd results. For example, gifted students might succeed on test scores, despite poor teaching.[35] These students, the court said, may have learned more with competent teachers. The court wrote:

> With primary reliance on these annual tests, however, it seems plausible that the system could end up teaching of and for the annual tests. Superior students who might have achieved their promise with competent teachers could go unfulfilled, and many students could end up being good at taking tests but inadequate in self-learning.[36]

Unfortunately, the court was required to focus on test results because of the statutory mandate. It was without jurisdiction to remedy this absurd result and wrote:

As a court we are not authorized to pass on the wisdom of these statutes—to rely instead on the wise alternative counsel of those who run this school district. When the meaning of a statute is plain, as here, our role is to enforce the law as written.[37]

If change was going to happen—if deference was going to be returned to the school administrator's judgment with respect to teacher performance—the state legislature was the appropriate forum, noted the court.[38]

Young v. Palm Beach County Board of Education[39]

Similarly, the case of *Young v. Palm Beach County Board of Education* demonstrates the impact of a statutory mandate requiring the use of student test scores on a district's termination case. In *Young* the district moved to terminate a poor performing teacher. The applicable statutes, like the case in *Sherrod*, required the district to consider student test scores in reaching its conclusion to terminate.[40] However, in *Young,* the school board's decision to terminate relied entirely on the principal's detailed description of performance deficiencies. The district did not consider test scores.

The court reversed the school board's decision. Like the case in *Sherrod*, the district's omission of student test data proved fatal to their case. Even in the face of well-detailed, documented evidence from the principal regarding poor performance, the termination decision could not be sustained. Wrote the court:

> Regardless of the good intentions of the School Board in relying on what it felt were suitable criteria to evaluate teacher performance, by depending on an assessment procedure not primarily based on student performance as measured by FCAT tests or local assessment, the School Board failed to follow the applicable law.[41]

Thus, the court had to follow the dictates of the statute that placed student test scores as the litmus test for teacher performance. Similar to *Sherrod*, the opinion of the administrators could not trump this omission, and this complicated the district's prospects.

Administrative Level Hearings: Canaries in the Coal Mine?

The impact of *Sherrod* and *Young* is rippling through other cases at the administrative law level in Florida. Some of these cases, discussed below, directly relate to the use of VAMs.[42]

Miami-Dade County School Board v. Hannibal Rosa[43]

In 2008, the Miami Florida School District moved to terminate teacher Hannibal Rosa.[44] Numerous visits and observations of Rosa's teaching supported the decision. For instance, in September of 2007, the school's assistant principal assessed Rosa using the district-wide observation form. She recorded that Rosa was deficient in numerous standards. Following the observation, school officials met with Rosa and discussed the deficiencies. Between September and October, the district provided Rosa with remedial assistance.[45]

Because of documented problems, the district placed Rosa on a ninety-day performance probation period. During this time, Rosa was observed but performance problems continued. School administrators provided remedial assistance during this time, again. They informed him that if his unsatisfactory teaching continued, he would be terminated.

Finally, in February of 2008, the district notified Rosa that it recommended to the school board that his employment be terminated based, among other things, on his poor evaluations.[46] In March of 2008, the board approved the recommendation. Mr. Rosa, as was his right, appealed the termination to the Florida Division of Administrative Hearings.

At the hearing, Mr. Rosa alleged that the district did not adhere to the requirements of the state's teacher evaluation law. That law required that poor performance evaluations "primarily consider" student performance on recognized state *annual* assessments.[47] The district countered that it complied with the statute because it considered results from the Dynamic Indicators of Basic Early Literacy Skills tests (DIBELS).[48] According to the district, Rosa's students did make satisfactory progress on the DIBELS.[49] Therefore, the district assumed that they complied with the statute and could justify their termination under the statute.

The administrative law judge (ALJ) rejected the district's argument. Indeed, it ruled that the DIBELS were not an appropriate assessment to evaluate a teacher's contribution under the statute. Even school district testimony concurred on this point; one school district official testified that the DIBELS were more of a "tool" to help teachers target their instruction. Instead, the evaluation statute required consideration based on *annual assessments*. For Rosa's evaluation, noted the court, this should have been student results on the Stanford Achievement Test.[50]

Because of this omission, Rosa was reinstated.[51] The *Rosa* ruling repeats the themes of the *Sherrod* and *Young,* and demonstrates their impact at the administrative level. Statutory requirements mandating evaluations based primarily on student progress as indicated by test scores can jeopardize a district's case in challenged adverse employment matters. And, more importantly, it required the decision-maker (here the ALJ) to ignore school administrators' observations and opinions about Rosa's teaching.

Miami-Dade County School Board v. Kristal

The *Kristal*[52] case is among the first cases in Florida, or any state, where the administrative law judge addressed the use of the state's VAM-model. Like the cases above, it demonstrates that VAMs complicate a school district's case. The facts, in brief, are as follows. The teacher, Elizabeth Kristal, had been employed as a teacher for fourteen (14) years. She taught at the Gulfstream School in the Miami-Dade school system from 2004–2005 until the 2012–2013 school year.

In November of 2013, the school principal moved to terminate Ms. Kristal. The principal observed Kristal on multiple occasions. She concluded that Kristal did not satisfy the district's evaluation standards, known as IPEGS (Instructional Performance Evaluation and Growth Systems). IPEGS consisted of eight (8) standards that constituted the minimum practices a teacher needed to demonstrate, and they were based on the state's recommendation for best evaluation practices.[53]

Four (4) of the IPEGS standards were observable through in-class observations and four (4) were considered "not observable" (e.g., instructional planning). Examples of nonobservable standards include: assessment of student performance by testing, data analysis, communication with parents, and behavior consistent with legal and ethical standards.

The principal concluded that Kristal's performance was deficient in all four of the *observable* standards under the IPEGS system. Moreover, she noted that Kristal had been given multiple opportunities to improve her practice (including tutorials with reading coaches) and had been placed on a growth plan, but her performance did not improve. The principal's recommendation for termination rested almost exclusively on her subjective, but professional, opinion of the teacher's in-class performance—the "observable" standards.

But, critically, the principal failed to consider Kristal's performance with respect to the *unobservable* standards related to student progress based on test data. At hearing, the ALJ noted that the principal's references to "data" were insufficient.[54]

The district's failure to account for test data doomed the district's case.[55] Florida law at that time required that at least 40 percent of [Kristal's] evaluation be based on data and indicators of student learning growth on annual assessments.[56] Here, the applicable test was the Stanford Achievement Test. According to the ALJ, the district failed to produce evidence concerning its weighing (or even consideration) required under the statute. Therefore, it could not sustain its charge that it had just cause to terminate Kristal based on its evaluations.[57]

To be sure, the termination was upheld but on other grounds. The district demonstrated it had cause to terminate the teacher under a different statute. That statute allows a finding of "just cause" if the district can demonstrate that the teacher is, among other things, "inefficient."[58] In this light, the district succeeded in demonstrating it had "just cause" to terminate. The facts illustrated that Ms. Kristal was inefficient because she was disorganized, failed to communicate with parents and students, generally failed to perform the duties of a teacher, and jeopardized the well-being and safety of her students.[59]

But, regardless, the *Kristal* case is a potential bellwether for districts eager to use VAMs and student test scores as a measure of teacher performance and termination. Here again, like the cases discussed earlier, the observations of the principal demonstrated an inefficient teacher, but because the district did not assess the student growth on tests, as required, the district's risk exposure (i.e., its chances of losing its case) increased.

KEY POINTS

- Historically, statutes and constitutions have vested school officials with considerable latitude in making personnel decisions. Because of this, courts defer to the judgment of local school officials on questions of teacher performance.

- Even when confronted with test scores, courts still emphasize and rely upon observations and testimony of school administrators, unless a statute requires them to look at other information (e.g., test scores).
- Put another way: prior to the advent of VAMs, local school officials had all the tools necessary to support their decisions regarding teacher employment and termination.
- The statutorily mandated use of VAMs has three primary impacts on court treatment of contested termination cases. First, courts *must consider* student achievement as assessed on standardized test scores and VAMs. Second, this requirement reduces court deference to school administrators' opinions. Third, taken together, these requirements increase the risk that districts may lose their cases; at the least, it complicates their efforts, especially at the state and administrative level.
- Several cases in Florida illustrate how VAMs reduce court deference to school officials and threaten a school district's decision and autonomy.

NOTES

1. *Sherrod v. Palm Beach County School Board,* 963 So.2d 251, 252 (Fla. Dist. Ct. App., 2006).

2. It is worth noting, again, that the author recognizes VAMs do not always reside in state standardized tests. However, for the most part, this has been where the development of these models has occurred.

3. Research regarding cases at the administrative level (i.e., those that are heard before the school board) does not receive sufficient attention, notwithstanding some efforts to correct this oversight. But see Mark Paige and Todd DeMitchell, "Arbitration Litigation Concerning Teacher Discipline for Misuse of Technology: A Preliminary Assessment," *West's Education Law Reporter* 296 (2013): 22–42.

4. Wisconsin Constitution, article X, sec. 3.

5. See, for example, Mass. Const. Pt. II, c. 5, section 2. See also, *McDuffy v. State,* 415 Mass. 545 (1993) (interpreting that provision as imposing an enforceable duty on the legislature to create and maintain a system of public schools).

6. To be sure, the landscape has shifted markedly. Indeed, many statutory shifts that mandate specific requirements in teacher evaluation suggest that legislatures believe they may have ceded too much discretion to local officials.

7. New Hampshire Rev. Stat. Ann. § 189:39 (2014).

8. See, for example, Conn. Stat. § 10–151 (b).

9. See, for example, Florida Stat. Ann. §§ 1012.22 and 1012.27 et seq. (describing the respective roles of the school boards and superintendents in hiring and dismissing teachers, among other personnel matters).

10. See, for example, Florida Stat. Ann. § 1012.23 (noting that the school board has authority over personnel matters, so long as it does not violate other laws or constitutions.).

11. A tenured teacher is one that has a continued expectation of employment. Because of this, when the state seeks to discontinue that employment, the teacher must have notice of that proposed action and an opportunity to dispute it through a hearing.

12. The statute has been amended to now require that the use of student growth on standardized tests be a determinant in a termination for incompetency or inefficiency. Conn. Gen. Stat. §§ 10-151(d) and 10-151b (2014) (requiring teacher evaluations to include student growth measures as assessed through standardized tests, where applicable).

13. Conn. Stat. § 10-151(d) (2014).

14. Ibid.

15. Ibid.

16. Conn Stat. § 4-183(j) (2014) (outlining the standards of reform for superior courts hearing appeals of administrative bodies, like school boards).

17. "Time Poll Results: Americans' Views on Teacher Tenure, Merit Pay and Other Educational Reforms," *Time*, September 9, 2010, accessed April 5, 2016, http://content.time.com/time/nation/article/0,8599,2016994,00.html.

18. Other states reflect this difference. In New Hampshire, a court cannot overturn a schoolboard's decision unless that decision is "clearly erroneous." See, for example, *In re Kennedy*, 162 N.H. 109 (2011) (affirming administrative hearing on grounds that the decision was not clearly erroneous).

19. *Whaley v. Anoka-Hennepin Iad. Sch. Dist.*, 325 N.W.2d 128 (Minn. 1982).

20. Ibid. at 132 (emphasis added).

21. Ibid.

22. *Johnson v. Francis Howell R-3 Bd. of Educ.*, 868 S.W.2d 191 (1994).

23. These terms are commonly seen in state tenure statutes as enumerated grounds to dismiss a tenured teacher.

24. *Johnson* at 193.

25. Ibid. at 195.

26. Ibid. at 199.

27. See, for example, *In re Proposed Termination of James E. Johnson's Teaching Contract,* 451 N.W.2d 343 (Minn. Ct. App. 1990) (upholding termination of tenured teacher based and considering, marginally, student test scores); see also *Brown v. Wood County Board of Education*, 184 W.Va. 205, 400 S.E.2d

213 (1990) (noting that absent an abuse of discretion, court would not interfere with school officials' judgment of teacher performance).

28. Ibid.

29. Specifically, the statute at issue in many of the cases discussed here required that student achievement on standardized tests be the "primary consideration" in a teacher's evaluation, where applicable. See, for example, *Sherrod v. Palm Beach County School Board,* 963 So.2d 251 (Fla. Dist. Ct. App., 2006). Current statutes require "[a]t least one-third percent of a performance evaluation must be based upon data and indicators of student learning growth assessed annually by statewide assessments." Florida Stat. Ann. § 1012.34 (2015).

30. *Sherrod,* supra, note 1.

31. In Florida, the process requires that the board bring formal charges to be heard before an administrative law judge (ALJ). The ALJ then recommended an order for discharge and the school board adopted that recommendation. The teacher appealed to the court, under which this case arose.

32. The statute has been amended and the word "primarily" has been removed. However, the primacy of student test scores has remained. Arguably, the legislature elevated the significance of student test scores when it mandated that *at least* 50 percent of the evaluation be comprised of student performance based on test scores, when applicable. Florida Stat. Ann. § 1012.34(3)(a)(1)(2014).

33. Fla. Stat. Ann. § 1012.34(3)(a) (2003).

34. *Sherrod v. Palm Beach County School Board,* supra, note 1, at 252.

35. Ibid. at 253.

36. Ibid.

37. Ibid.

38. The *Sherrod* decision emerged in another opinion on the same matter. In the case of *Young v. Palm Beach County School Board,* the Florida District Court of Appeals found that the school board's decision did not satisfy the substantial evidence test precisely because the board failed to follow the statutory requirement to consider student performance on tests scores. See note 40, infra.

39. Ibid.

40. *Young v. Palm Beach County School Board,* 968 So.2d 38 (Fla. Dist. Ct. App., 2006).

41. Ibid. at 39.

42. Florida Stat. Ann. § 1012.34 et seq. (2013).

43. *Miami-Dade County Sch. Bd. v. Hannibal Rosa,* 2008 WL 5266661 (Fla. Div. Admin. Hrgs., Case No. 08-1495, December 16, 2008).

44. Mr. Rosa was not a tenured teacher. However, because the district moved to terminate him during the life of his contract, due process protections applied. Thus, his case contains similar legal issues and is included as part of this discussion.

45. *Miami v. Rosa*, supra, note 43, at *3.
46. Ibid. at *5.
47. Ibid. at *10–11 (citations omitted).
48. Ibid. at *6.
49. Ibid. at *7–8.
50. Ibid. at *11.
51. Ibid. at *12.
52. *School Board of Miami-Dade County v. Elizabeth Kristal*, (Fla. Div. Admin. Hrg., case no. 13-0447), note 41. Significantly, the *Kristal* case was decided under Florida's current evaluation requirements that include the use of a more refined process for VAMs.
53. Ibid. at *11.
54. Ibid. at fn. 9. "The context in which the term [data] is used seems to suggest [that it did not reflect student test scores.]"
55. Ibid. "[The District"] did not present evidence regarding the relative weight assigned to the test scores in evaluating Respondent—a fatal flaw to the charged under [the state's evaluation laws]."
56. Ibid. at *18. Florida state law required that at least 50 percent of a performance-based evaluation be based on data. However, in situations like Ms. Kristal's, if less than three years of data are available, the years of data must be used and the percentage can be no less than 40 percent of the evaluation.
57. Ibid. at *20. "Based on the findings of fact, [School District], did not prove by a preponderance of evidence that [Kristal] failed to correct performance deficiencies such that her employment should be terminated pursuant to [the teacher evaluation procedures.]"
58. Ibid. at *20 (citations omitted).
59. Ibid.

5

VAMs, COLLECTIVE BARGAINING, AND ARBITRATION

More Legal Headaches for Administrators?

> I think if there is one thing I have learned over the last 15 months, it's that cooperation, collaboration, and consensus building are way overrated.
>
> —Michelle Rhee[1]

In 2010, Washington, DC, school superintendent Michelle Rhee fired 241 teachers because they failed to satisfy expectations under the district's new teacher evaluation system, IMPACT.[2] Simultaneously, she notified another 700 teachers that they faced termination unless their IMPACT ratings improved.[3] IMPACT relied heavily on VAMs.

The Washington teachers union explored various legal options to challenge Rhee's decision.[4] Ultimately, they pursued a remedy under the applicable collective bargaining agreement (CBA) "grievance arbitration" clause, rather than through the courts. Specifically, the union contended that the administration failed to follow evaluations procedures under the CBA. The administration, therefore, breached the agreement.

By way of background, bargaining plays an important role in education and the day-to-day operation of public schools. Through this process—which culminates in a negotiated agreement (the CBA)—local stakeholders determine the terms and processes of their working conditions. Importantly, as discussed below in greater detail with reference to

Washington, DC, a CBA provides for a process to resolve disputes that arise between employers and employees. This is known as final and binding arbitration.

This chapter discusses the impact of VAMs in the context of collective bargaining. First, the legal framework of collective bargaining in evaluation is presented. Second, the limiting impact of VAMs on the ability of unions and administrators to craft evaluation mechanisms at the bargaining table is highlighted.[5] Third, the chapter notes the way in which unions have used collective bargaining tools—particularly final and binding arbitration—to resist implementation of recent evaluation changes.

Washington, DC, is highlighted in this chapter. There the district prescribed a VAM-based evaluation system for employment decisions. Unions, largely excluded from the evaluation design, have sought to protect their membership against implementation of the evaluation system. Importantly, they have used arbitration provisions in the CBA to this end. Arbitration is a unique dispute resolution mechanism with important distinctions from court litigation.[6] At the moment, the DC school districts and unions are mired in arbitration and court challenges.

Washington is a bellwether and deserves examination. In this light, many districts may rethink their reliance on VAMs. To begin with, it illustrates the toxicity that develops when central office administrators unilaterally implement *any* major policy initiative without feedback from teachers. In addition, the case study of Washington demonstrates how unions can effectively use arbitration to challenge unilateral action regarding evaluation and frustrate (rightfully, in the case of VAMs) a district's efforts.

THE LEGAL FRAMEWORK OF COLLECTIVE BARGAINING

Before discussing events in Washington, it is necessary to consider some of collective bargaining's essential purposes and parameters. To begin with, collective bargaining allows school boards and unions to negotiate terms of employment with one another. The process culminates with a collective bargaining agreement (CBA), a legally binding document. In essence, the CBA is a "contract." Both parties are bound by its terms.

Collective bargaining promotes workplace stability. It sets the terms of work and expectations. It creates agreed-upon rules to efficiently manage and resolve disputes. If either party believes the CBA has been violated, they can file a grievance.[7] Most grievances are resolved through a multistep process that ends in "final and binding arbitration." Because, in theory, arbitration is *final and binding*, the parties can effectively resolve disputes without resorting to costly court litigation. In sum, collective bargaining creates a "system of industrial self-government."[8]

Collective bargaining is a creature of statute. In other words, it is not a right. Rather, a state legislature can allow (or prohibit) collective bargaining. Forty-five (45) states allow collective bargaining.[9] In these states, school officials and unions *must* negotiate "in good faith" over proposals *primarily* related to "wages, hours and terms and conditions" of employment (e.g., a proposal to increase salaries by 5 percent).[10]

The scope of bargaining—the spectrum of issues that can be discussed at the table—is important to consider when discussing collective bargaining of teacher evaluation. To be "bargainable" (i.e., discussed and negotiated at the table) a subject must be within the "scope of bargaining." Indeed, various education topics are classified as one of the following subjects: mandatory, prohibited, or permissive. Districts and unions are not required to bargain every proposal (i.e., those that are *not* primarily related to wages, hours, and conditions of employment).

Some examples illustrate bargaining scope. Let's assume that a union proposes to raise base wages by 5 percent. That's a proposal that primarily relates to "wages" and, therefore, is a *mandatory* subject of bargaining. The proposal must be negotiated, but neither side is compelled to accept the proposal.

However, let's assume that a union proposes to reduce the school year to 100 days rather than the 185 days as required by statute. Further assume that a state statute, as is the case in many places, requires that every school year be no less than 185 days. The union proposal conflicts with the statute. Thus, the proposal is a *prohibited subject* of bargaining because the state statute trumps any bargaining agreement. In other words, the sides *cannot* entertain these proposals or codify them in the CBA.

Permissive subjects of bargaining fall in a grey area. With respect to permissive subjects, the parties *may* bargain the issue at their discretion. Another example demonstrates subjects that may fall under this category. Let's assume that a school district is considering offering a particular math curriculum. Typically, a school district could unilaterally implement a curriculum, but they *may* discuss that decision with the unions. Thus, the decision of a particular curriculum is *permissive*.[11]

Is teacher evaluation a mandatory, permissive, or prohibited subject of bargaining? In brief, it depends. The scope of bargaining of *teacher evaluation* varies by states. In some states, teacher evaluation is prohibited. Unions and management cannot—even if they both wanted to—negotiate the subject. In others, teacher evaluation is a *mandatory subject* of bargaining. Here, the parties *must* entertain proposals on the topic. Yet, in still others, the subject appears to be at least a *permissive subject*; school boards *can* negotiate the topic at their discretion.[12]

To be sure, the role, if any, of collective bargaining in education is contested.[13] There are two polar sides in this debate. On the one hand, some believe collective bargaining should *not* be permitted at all. They argue that bargaining allows unions undue influence over the direction and maintenance of schools. In this light, bargaining allows unions to put the interests of employees over children. Moreover, they argue that bargaining is undemocratic because it provides teachers unions with a disproportionate amount of power over elected school officials.

On the other hand, bargaining can be a positive force. Unions and teachers can leverage bargaining to create reforms and innovation that benefit schools. Collective bargaining allows unions to improve working conditions, for example, and that benefits children. Increasing pay improves morale. In sum, the unions' and the children's interests are mutually reinforcing. Thus, bargaining serves multi purposes and shared interests of constituencies.

Impact of VAMs on Collective Bargaining

VAMs have had a diluting impact on the ability to bargain teacher evaluation, particularly in states where evaluation is a mandatory or permitted topic. More specifically, VAMs restrict local administrators' ability to jointly craft evaluation processes with teacher representatives.[14] For example, when a statute requires that VAMs (or student growth measures) *must* constitute a specific portion of a teacher's evaluation (e.g., a percent of a rating), local stakeholders *cannot* negotiate away that requirement. This portion of evaluation is, effectively, a prohibited subject.

The case of Massachusetts illustrates this limiting nature. In that state, the legislature classifies evaluation as a mandatory subject of bargaining by statute. In other words, proposals related to the topic *must* be negotiated. However, Massachusetts's evaluation law *also requires* that student growth measures be included in evaluations. Thus, this component of evaluation is effectively *prohibited;* unions and managements cannot evade this requirement through the bargaining process.

The legal mandates of VAMs restrict local control because they place nonnegotiable requirements on districts regarding the use of evaluations in employment decisions, as well. In Florida, statutes require that significant employment decisions *must* be made with reference to evaluations that, in turn, rely heavily on VAM ratings. Unions and management cannot negotiate any compromise with this requirement if they believe it is unfair. By virtue of the statute, they are stuck with the end result.[15]

To be sure, unions and management can continue to negotiate other significant aspects of evaluations. This includes the following: the procedure of evaluations, particulars about classroom visits for evaluation purposes (e.g., announced or unannounced, the quantity of visits to be used in evaluations), and data that can be used. Thus, while the VAM mandate has narrowed the scope of evaluation bargaining, there remain some important points for discussion at the bargaining table.[16]

Unfortunately, when unions are excluded from important policy matters (like the use of student test scores in evaluation) they are more aggressive in protecting their remaining rights under the CBA. For example, they are more inclined to strictly interpret the CBA and demand the district follow it "to the letter." In this process, unions can—and do—pursue violations of the CBA grievance arbitration. This is significant because arbitration may be a "friendlier forum" for challenges to VAM-based evaluations, as discussed below.

ARBITRATION: A MORE FAVORABLE VENUE FOR CHALLENGES TO TEACHER EVALUATION?

Thus far, this book has considered *court-based* challenges to VAMs both at the federal and state levels. Yet there are other forums of law to resolve disputes, including grievance arbitration. By way of background, in the course of implementing a collective bargaining agreement (CBA), disputes frequently arise over the application of the CBA. Accordingly, many CBAs provide for final binding arbitration to resolve the dispute.

Arbitration is a less formal, less costly forum to settle remedies as compared to seeking a court remedy. But, generally, the process provides for an expeditious dispute resolution process that promotes industrial peace.[17]

Moreover, arbitration decisions are difficult to overturn on appeal.[18] One state court stated this proposition as follows:

> It is the policy of the law to favor and encourage arbitration and every reasonable intendment will be indulged to give effect to such proceedings and to favor the regularity and integrity of the arbitrator's acts.[19]

Thus, only under limited exceptions, should a court overturn (or vacate) an arbitrator's award. This means that, outside a few exceptions, the parties will abide by this decision.

An arbitrator's authority is confined, however, and far from absolute. Importantly, they must adhere to the terms of CBA; they are, in the final analysis, the interpreter of the agreement. Consequently, their decisions must be grounded to specific provisions of the CBA. They cannot fashion their own version of "industrial justice" and decide matters as they would like or go beyond the intent of the contract. An arbitrator may look for guidance from sources beyond the CBA, but the award must "draw its essence" from the agreement.[20]

Yet an arbitrator is an expert of sorts, with considerable knowledge about workplace issues. Courts have noted that arbitrators are well versed in the "common law of the shop." The U.S. Supreme Court has said that:

> The labor arbitrator's source of law is not confined to the express provisions of the contract. . . . The parties expect that his judgment of a particular grievance will reflect not only what the contract says but, insofar as the collective bargaining agreement permits, *such factors as the effect upon productivity of a particular result, its consequence to the morale of the shop, his judgment whether tensions will be heightened or diminished.*[21] (emphasis added).

Given this, she does have some discretion, especially on issues relative to employee productivity. Thus, the parties expect that an arbitrator will be able to use her discretion to fashion an award that ultimately promotes labor peace.

The concepts of worker productivity and morale may be factors relevant to an arbitrator's ultimate decision.[22] This is an important point in relation to cases involving VAMs. As discussed in prior chapters, VAMs negatively impact school cultures and, like other high-stakes regimens, can undercut morale. As arbitrators hear cases involving VAMs, they can—and perhaps should—consider this impact. At the very least, it is important to note that the arbitration context appears to allow for this possibility, within certain limits.

Arbitration may also be more favorable to employees, as opposed to courts. Scholars have noted that a number of features of arbitration contribute to a higher win rate for unions in that context.[23] For instance, procedural devices typically used by employers, like motions to dismiss, are less likely to be used in arbitration.[24] Costs for arbitration are lower than court litigation. Unlike court litigation, non-lawyers can represent employees in arbitration. In sum, unions have—and will—use arbitration to improve their chances of succeeding in employment disputes, especially those related to VAMs, where applicable.[25]

GRIEVANCE ARBITRATION, TEACHER EVALUATION, AND VAMs: THE WASHINGTON, DC, EXAMPLE

There are some early indications that unions are effectively using arbitration—as is their right—to challenge employment decisions based on VAMs. Events in Washington, DC, illustrate this point. That city's unions and teachers have been mired in arbitration—which has turned into court litigation—since the district began linking VAMs to high-stakes employment decisions. Events in Washington should give pause to policymakers and administrators seeking to unilaterally implement VAMs—and use them for high-stakes employment matters.

Indeed, the case of Washington exemplifies the unintended consequences of prescriptive reforms on high-stakes issues, especially where teachers are excluded from the design process.[26] As noted above, the superintendent at the time, Michelle Rhee, viewed collaboration as "overrated," thus setting the tone and clear lines of authority. Even assuming Ms. Rhee was well-intentioned with respect to her unilateral actions, her IMPACT evaluations system caused considerable disruption in the district. At the very least, it requires us to ask: is the cost of mandating VAMs in teacher evaluations worth their questionable benefit?

By way of brief background, in 2009–2010, the DC Public Schools implemented a new evaluation system known as IMPACT. The instrument used in IMPACT reflected a VAM-based approach to teacher evaluation. Specifically, it used student test scores to evaluate teachers and used those evaluations to make high-stakes employment decisions. IMPACT also linked increased compensation to evaluator ratings.

At the end of 2009–2010, ninety-four teachers were rated "ineffective" and were separated from the district. An additional 670 teachers were rated "minimally effective" and given one probationary year to demonstrate improvement or face separation.

The teachers union challenged the district's application of the evaluation procedures under the collective bargaining agreement. The applicable CBA provided that the "evaluation process" was subject to the grievance and arbitration process.[27] Importantly, the CBA explicitly excluded from negotiations and arbitration the actual rating of a teacher. But compliance with the process was subject to grievance arbitration.

The union made several specific charges against the district. It contended that IMPACT used "unreliable data in assessing" teacher performance.[28] Moreover, it pled that the IMPACT system violated the CBA because it set "unclear expectations" and "failed to consider" other relevant factors in a teacher's evaluation. Thus, the district failed to follow a fair process in its evaluations. As a remedy, the union sought to have the evaluation ratings expunged from teachers' records and back pay for those teachers who lost employment as a result of the ratings.[29] It also sought to have the ratings changed to "effective."

The district disagreed that the issue was subject to arbitration. They argued that the ultimate evaluative judgment or rating (ineffective, or effective, etc.) was the district's prerogative. In other words, it was beyond the scope of the arbitrator because, in essence, rating teachers is a management prerogative. Thus, the district contended that the union was attempting to usurp the school district's authority.

The district brought the issue—whether the union's claim was subject to arbitration—to court. That court noted that an arbitrator could, indeed, hear the issue of whether the district violated the processes of the evaluation. The court held that the parties agreed to these processes and, therefore, both were bound to follow them. The case is currently on appeal.

Regardless of the outcome on appeal, the Washington example demonstrates another legal forum for disputing the use of VAMs: final and binding arbitration. It also reflects how unions will—and perhaps should—use rights under the collective bargaining agreement to advocate for fair evaluation systems.

OTHER EXAMPLES: USING ARBITRATION TO CHALLENGE EVALUATIONS

Even though they do not involve VAMs per se, cases in other jurisdictions also demonstrate the potential use of arbitration as a means to challenge employment decisions based on evaluations generally. For example, in *Board of Education, Bellmore-Merrick Central High School District v. Bellmore-Merrick United Secondary Teachers, Inc.*, an arbitrator ordered the reinstatement of a probationary teacher where the district failed to follow specified evaluation procedures.[30] In this case, pursuant to terms of the CBA, the teacher was supposed to be informed of parental complaints and given an opportunity to refute them.

However, the district failed to follow this procedure and nonrenewed the teacher. The union challenged this violation of procedure and argued that the appropriate remedy was reinstatement. The case ultimately was appealed to the state's highest court where the arbitrator's order was upheld.[31] Similar cases mirror the *Bellmore* case whereby the decision to terminate employment has effectively been overturned at the arbitration level.[32]

In Massachusetts, a string of cases also illustrate this point. For example, in *School Committee of Danvers v. Tyman* the applicable CBA required the district to abide by certain procedures typical in many CBAs.[33] That CBA required that a teacher receive notice of negative material in their file and an opportunity to respond to it.[34] In *Danvers* the state's highest court ruled that the issue in the case—whether the district followed the arbitration—was subject to arbitration.[35] Importantly, the court noted that an arbitrator could reinstate a teacher on a probationary basis because of a district's failure to follow these procedures.

To be sure, there are some caveats with respect to arbitration challenges to evaluation procedures. To begin with, an award for reinstatement could only be for a time-period "sufficient for the school board to reevaluate the teacher in accordance with the prescribed procedures."[36] It could not lead to tenure. Moreover, not all states permit reinstatement as a remedy because of procedural violations.[37] However, importantly, procedural violations can lead to costly arbitration proceedings. This complicates a nonrenewal or termination decision.[38] At the very least, it requires more resources to defend. As we see school districts making more decisions based on VAMs, it is likely we will also see more challenges based on procedural violations of the collective bargaining agreement.

The Paradox of Public Sector Labor Law and the VAM Mandate

The events in Washington illustrate what has been described as a "paradox in public sector labor law" and teacher evaluation, in particular.[39] The paradox is this: although excluding the unions from evaluation design and implementation *appears* to give a district more freedom to unilaterally implement their ideas, quite the opposite happens. This is what happened in Washington, DC, where unions have aggressively sought to halt implementation of the idea. Excluding unions promotes an "us versus them" mindset that is not conducive to workplace harmony.

Yet had unions been included in developing the evaluation system from the beginning, they could have worked with management to design a system that reflected a thoughtful use of VAMs. Unions would have "buy-in" to see the evaluation succeed. In other words, including them would have likely resulted in union cooperation. At the very minimum, they would not have viewed management as the adversary.

More importantly, collective bargaining could provide an opportunity for unions and management to apply their collective wisdom to an issue of teacher evaluation. But because of the requirements that VAMs must (by statute) occupy a significant portion of an evaluation, application of local knowledge and expertise is diminished.[40]

KEY POINTS

- The introduction of VAMs impacts, to some extent, the ability of teachers and administrators to use collective bargaining to fashion local solutions to local problems.

- The unilateral and prescriptive nature of VAMs isolates teachers from the development of evaluation systems.
- "Final and binding arbitration" is an alternative dispute resolution process that may be a more favorable forum for those seeking to challenge VAM-based decisions.
- Recent arbitration and litigation in Washington, DC, illustrates how VAMs can contribute to an acrimonious relationship between teachers and administrators.
- Excluding teachers and unions from bargaining in important components of evaluation incentivizes unions to use provisions in the collective bargaining agreement to thwart the implementation of those evaluations.
- Including teachers and unions, as discussed in the following chapter, gives unions a vested interest in evaluation systems and may contribute to their successful implementation.

NOTES

1. Richard Kahlenberg, "Gov. Scott Walker can thank Michelle Rhee for making teachers unions the enemy," *The Washington Post*, February 27, 2011, accessed December 15, 2015, www.washingtonpost.com/wp-dyn/content/article/2011/02/25/AR2011022503246.html.

2. Sally Holland, "D.C. School System Fires 241 Teachers," *CNN*, July 23, 2010, accessed November 5, 2015, www.cnn.com/2010/US/07/23/district.of.columbia.teachers.fired/.

3. Ibid.

4. Bill Turque, "D.C., Teachers in Court Fight over Evaluations," *The Washington Post*, July 1, 2011, accessed November 5, 2015, www.washingtonpost.com/local/education/dc-teachers-in-court-fight-over-evaluations/2011/06/30/AGqPvitH_story.html.

5. Chapter 6 discusses how administrators can embrace some tools to mitigate this impact, especially in the context of collective bargaining.

6. See, for example, *Dennis-Yarmouth Regional School Committee v. Dennis Teachers Association,* 372 Mass 116 (1977).

7. An sample definition of grievance is: "[A] claim based upon an event or condition which affects the wages, hours, or conditions of employment of a teacher or group of teachers and/or the interpretation, meaning, or application of any of the provisions of this Agreement or any subsequent agreement entered

pursuant to this Agreement." *School Committee of Danvers v. Tyman,* 372 Mass. 106, fn. 2 (1977).

8. *United Steelworkers of America v. Warrior & Gulf Navigation Co.*, 363 U.S. 574, 580 (1960).

9. Milla Sanes and John Schmitt, *Regulation of Public Sector Collective Bargaining in the States* (Washington, DC: Center for Economic Policy and Research, 2014).

10. See, for example, N.H. Rev. Stat. Ann. § 273-A:3 (2014) and M.G.L. c.150E-6 (2014).

11. However, importantly, the *impact* of that decision will likely lead to negotiations. Indeed, the decision to adopt a curriculum will no doubt require teachers to participate in training or gain additional professional development requiring teachers to put in more time at work. These *impacts* primarily relate to wages, hours, and conditions of employment and, therefore, issues in this area *must* be negotiated.

12. The benefits of bargaining evaluation and education policy in general have been discussed in other forums. See note 13, infra.

13. For an overview of the sides of bargaining in education, see Mark Paige, "Applying the 'Paradox' Theory: A Law and Policy Analysis of Collective Bargaining Rights and Teacher Evaluation," *Brigham Young Journal of Law and Education* (Spring 2013): 21–43.

14. The discussion generally relates to states where collective bargaining is permissible. However, it has some relevance in places where collective bargaining is impermissible. In those states, unions and administrators often "meet and confer" about significant policy decisions.

15. To be sure, they can lobby their state legislature to amend the statute. However, bargaining allows for a nimble process to remediate shortcomings in the near term. This is discussed in chapter 6.

16. The significance of this is discussed in greater detail in chapter 6 where collective bargaining is presented as a potential solution to the issues created by overly prescriptive evaluation policies.

17. *United Steelworkers v. Warrior & Gulf*, 363 U.S. 574, 578 (1960).

18. Where applicable, most states provide for a right of appeal to a state court. See, for example, M.G.L. c.71, 42 (noting that an arbitration award is subject to judicial review).

19. *Mahoning County Board of Mental Retardation and Developmental Disabilities v. Mahoning County TMR Education Association*, 22 Ohio St. 3d 80, 83–84, 488 N.E.2d 872, 875 (1986) (citing *Campbell v. Automatic Die & Products Co.*, 162 Ohio St. 321, 329, 123 N.E.2d 401, 405 [1954]).

20. Ibid.

21. See, note 22, *United Steelworkers v. Warrior & Gulf*, at 582.

22. Ibid.

23. See note 25, infra.

24. Michael Green, "Debunking the Myth of Employer Advantage from Using Mandatory Arbitration for Discrimination Claims," *Rutgers Law Journal* 31 (2000): 399–471: 470.

25. See, for example, Alexander J. S. Colvin and Kelly Pike, "Saturns and Rickshaws Revisited: What Kind of Employment Arbitration System has Developed?" *Ohio State Journal on Dispute Resolution* 29 (2014): 78 (noting that where employees are represented in arbitration by unions, their win rate improves).

26. The author is stretching to give the benefit of the doubt to the prior superintendent Michelle Rhee who seemed to view teachers as enemies rather than partners.

27. Collective Bargaining Agreement between the Washington Teachers' Union and the District of Columbia Public Schools (2007–2012), § 15.3.

28. *Washington Teachers' Union v. District of Columbia Public Schools*, 77 A.3d 441 (D.C. 2013).

29. Ibid.

30. *Board of Education, Bellmore-Merrick Central High School District v. Bellmore-Merrick United Secondary Teachers, Inc.*, 39 N.Y.2d 167 (1976).

31. To be sure, the court recognized that an arbitrator could not issue an award that would result in the teacher receiving tenure. By way of statute in that state, only a school district could award tenure. However, the court noted that an arbitrator did have the authority to fashion an award (e.g., reinstatement *without* tenure) that could preserve the school committee's prerogative and be an appropriate remedy for the CBA violation. In this regard, the teacher could teach in the following year and be evaluated pursuant to the relevant procedures.

32. For example, the Massachusetts Supreme Judicial Court has issued numerous cases standing for this proposition. See, for example, *School Committee of Danvers v. Tyman*, 372 Mass. 106 (1977), *Dennis-Yarmouth Regional School Committee v. Dennis Teachers Association*, 372 Mass. 116 (1977).

33. *Dennis-Yarmouth v. Dennis Teachers*, 372 Mass. 106 (1977).

34. Ibid. at 107.

35. See also, *School Committee of West Bridgewater v. West Bridgewater Teachers' Association*, 372 Mass. 121 (1977); *Dennis-Yarmouth v. Dennis Teachers,* 372 Mass. 116 (1977).

36. *Danvers v. Tyman* at 111.

37. See *Jones v. Wrangell School District*, 696 P.2d 677, 679 (Alaska 1985); see also *North Beach Education Association v. North Beach School District,* 639 P.2d 821 (1982) (allowing for an arbitrator to craft remedies short of reinstatement); and *Illinois Education Association Local Community High School Dis-*

trict 218 v. Board of Education of School District 218, Cook County, 62 Ill.2d 127, 130–131 (1975).

38. Arbitration is a less costly dispute resolution than court challenges. However, it is not inexpensive and, in some instances, the losing party must pay the arbitration costs for *both* sides.

39. See, Martin Malin, "The Paradox of Public Sector Labor Law," *Indiana Law Journal* 84, no. 4 (2009): 1369–1399, and Mark Paige, "Applying the 'Paradox' Theory: A Law and Policy Analysis of Collective Bargaining Rights and Teacher Evaluation," *Brigham Young Journal of Law and Education* (Spring 2013): 21–43.

40. However, as discussed in the following chapter, it is not completely removed. There continue to exist some methods by which local officials may be able to strategically mitigate this impact.

6

COLLECTIVE BARGAINING

A Tool to Mitigate VAM Damage to School Culture

> The American Labor Movement has consistently demonstrated its devotion to the public interest. It is, and has been, good for all America.
> —John F. Kennedy

In the spring of 2015, Fulton County Superior Court judge Jerry Baxter sentenced nine Atlanta public educators to jail for conspiring to inflate students' standardized test scores.[1] He noted a pervasive cheating culture that cut across the school system and flowed directly from the superintendent's office.[2] Judge Baxter commented that the scandal was "like the sickest thing that has ever happened in this town."[3]

Atlanta is not an isolated incident. Similar scandals have occurred across the country.[4] The United States Government Accountability Office (GAO) reported numerous incidents in other states.[5] That *some* teachers and schools are engaged in cheating, at the very least, requires us to scrutinize the high-stakes accountability policies that encourage such behavior.

Accountability based on high-stakes testing carries risks.[6] Punitive systems based on standardized tests encourage educators to press ethical, if not legal, limits. The daughter of Reverend Martin Luther King Jr., in reflecting on the Atlanta scandal, was quoted as follows:

Teachers are under tremendous pressure to meet standards and ensure that students pass tests, even to the extent that their jobs, their livelihoods may be threatened.[7]

Echoing this theme, one scholar summarized the high-stakes accountability atmosphere in education as follows:

Given the importance of test scores, it is not surprising that teachers and school officials have devised various ways of gaming the testing system: that is, tricks and shortcuts to achieve the desired results, without improving education.[8]

But, even in the face of Atlanta and these warnings, the high-stakes accountability drive continues. VAMs extend this trend and will perpetuate this collateral damage.

Because VAMs will diminish and add toxins to a school culture, they will ultimately minimize student success at the building level. Yet, as noted, school administrators *must* (in many states) use VAMs to evaluate and terminate. This mandate puts school administrators in an untenable position. They must make employment and evaluative decisions based on principles they know undercut positive learning cultures. How can school administrators balance these competing, and conflicting, demands?

This chapter outlines practical steps for school administrators facing these challenges. It returns to the subject of chapter 5—collective bargaining. In fact, the chapter recommends that local education stakeholders use collective bargaining to mitigate the desultory effects of VAMs, especially as they relate to school culture. To be sure, as discussed in the prior chapter, VAMs have reduced some of the inherent local power available through collective bargaining. Yet, collective bargaining, *if harnessed in specific ways*, can still blunt some of the negative impact of VAMs.

The chapter is organized as follows. The first section outlines the importance of school culture on student achievement; it pays specific attention to a promising tool in teacher professional development: professional learning communities (PLCs).[9] Unfortunately, as discussed in the second section of the chapter, the very attributes we promote through PLCs are threatened by high-stakes VAM-based evaluations. However, the third portion of the chapter identifies ways that collective bargaining[10] can be leveraged to insulate schools from the negative consequences of VAMs.[11]

The chapter concludes that, where possible, local administrators and educators should collaboratively implement a two-pronged approach. First, they should adopt a *particular method of bargaining* (interest-based bargaining, or IBB). Second, they should use IBB to ensure the codification of a *particular method of evaluation* (peer-assisted review, or PAR) in the bargaining agreement. Both methods require collaboration among all relevant stakeholders.

SCHOOL CULTURE AND STUDENT ACHIEVEMENT

A positive culture is vital to an organization's success. Private sector companies understand this link. Thoughtful private sector business leaders are aware that "[t]he culture of an enterprise plays a dominant role in exemplary performance."[12] The notion of a workplace culture features prominently in "business lexicon."[13] It is almost axiomatic that a healthy work environment—where employees feel challenged and included—leads to increased productivity.

These same general rules apply to public schools. Students achieve when local education stakeholders share a common goal and work together. Numerous benefits accrue to schools and districts focusing on this link. A healthy culture promotes the following:

1. School effectiveness and productivity;
2. Collegiality, collaboration, communication, and problem-solving practices;
3. Innovation and school improvement;
4. Commitment and motivation;
5. Energy of school, staff, students, and community; and
6. Focus of attention on what is important and valued.[14]

Specific Attributes of Positive School Cultures

Certain qualities can be identified in schools with positive cultures. First, teachers share responsibility for every student, not just those they teach every day. Schools that break down the isolating walls between teachers create a sense of larger purpose among staff and promote collaboration. Moreover, educators value and need collegiality to sustain themselves as professionals and contribute to their students' growth.[15]

Second, successful schools encourage teachers to take difficult teaching assignments. This is especially significant in high-needs schools, where the best teachers are in the highest demand. In these contexts, teachers that assume tough assignments should not fear job reprisals if they are not successful. If that is the case, they will be dissuaded from tackling these challenging positions. Indeed, attaching a continued employment to value-added scores in high-needs districts will only deepen the teacher shortage.[16]

Third, successful schools evaluate teachers fairly. This makes intuitive sense. No organization—private or public—would survive if employees believed their performance was arbitrarily assessed. If that is the case, employees would seek work elsewhere. But a sense of a fairness in workplace evaluation and treatment attracts and retains educators.

Finally, successful schools share governance. Teachers want to problem-solve issues related to their schools. Importantly, they have expertise that can add value to most problems confronting schools. Shared governance vests teachers in the problem and the solution. For these reasons, shared governance of schools (e.g., site-based management) has been noted as a marker of a successful school.

Promoting Positive School Culture with Professional Learning Communities (PLCs)

Professional learning communities (PLCs) have been identified as a particular tool that can be used to promote all the attributes of a positive school culture. PLCs are widely believed to be the most successful professional development tool available to schools in great part because of their collaborative nature.[17] Collaborative frameworks, of which PLCs are a leading example, improve teacher quality.[18]

But, importantly, VAMs threaten PLCs. The school cultural qualities required for PLCs are in direct conflict with those currently promoted by VAMs. Professional learning communities, generally speaking, are semiformal structures where teachers exchange instructional best practices.[19] These communities share an "undeviating focus on student learning."[20] A defining characteristic is a community focused on improving the success of every student.[21]

PLCs are "public" forums. Teachers openly share instructional ideas, successes, and failures. This builds camaraderie and taps local education expertise. PLCs "break down the walls of isolation and privacy that characterize schools."[22] This significance cannot be understated. Teachers have considerable knowledge about instructional practices and PLCs provide a spigot for this information to flow freely.

Collaboration is a cornerstone of PLCs. Through PLCs teachers engage in "deliberate and intentional act[s] of collaborating to analyze student achievement."[23] This collective effort improves morale.[24] This impact cannot be understated. Organizations succeed or fail, in large part, based on the internal level of collaboration.

BAM! VAMs NEGATIVE IMPACT ON SCHOOL CULTURE

The very elements that create a positive school culture—specifically reflected in PLCs—are directly threatened by high-stakes accountability evaluation systems such as VAMs.[25] The hyper-focus on testing results as indicators of outcomes and teacher value leads to a host of pernicious impacts on school culture that are in direct affront to PLCs. These include:

- Increased levels of "cheating" by school administrators or educators to boost test scores, thus creating a rule-breaking culture.
- Motivation, especially in choice or charter contexts, to exclude higher needs students, thus creating a culture of exclusion rather than inclusion.
- Increased use of legal mechanisms (e.g., the Americans with Disabilities Act [ADA] or the Individuals with Disabilities Education Act [IDEA]) as means to obtain testing accommodations; thus, using the law in ways that conflict with its intent.
- A narrowing of curricula focus (and resource allocation) to only those subjects that are "tested" for high-stakes purposes (e.g., math or reading); thus excluding teachers and students from equal educational opportunity.

- Veteran teachers affirmatively seeking out the less needy student, leaving the higher needs students with novice teachers.

VAMs, as used in high-stakes evaluations, exacerbate these effects. First, to begin with, they disincentive teachers from collaborating. Because the ratings are relative to fellow teachers, teachers are, in fact, encouraged to covet their best instructional ideas. Under these "zero-sum" game rules, teachers are certain to retreat to their own classrooms. Expressing a similar theme, one researcher stated:

> [T]eachers with the strongest overall knowledge and skills might well reclaim their students and conduct all instruction within a self-contained class, leaving less experienced and less effective teachers to cope on their own.[26]

In sum, teachers evaluated under VAM-heavy systems will shift from collaboration to individualization. Based on what we know about PLCs and the positive force of collaboration, this is disconcerting.

Second, and in a related point, VAMs will increase turnover. The literature on this point is clear. When teachers work in isolation or do not feel part of a greater organization, there are higher rates of turnover. In turn, turnover contributes to a lack of stability and impacts student achievement.

Third, VAMs will lead to a balkanization of school subject disciplines. As noted, VAMs create a hierarchy of subject areas based on the subjects most closely associated with high-stakes decisions (math and reading). Because of this, these areas (and teachers) will certainly capture more resources and attention than other non-tested subjects. This effect simply continues a narrowing of curriculum that already is occurring.[27]

Finally, and perhaps most troubling, a continued use of a flawed evaluation mechanism fuels a sense of workplace injustice. In particular, it suggests that administration is willing—and able—to employ deeply suspect evaluation means which only engenders suspicion on all sides. Education professionals already recognize that VAMs are statistically flawed; their efforts to overturn VAM implementation in the courts reflect this sense of wrong. Furthermore, continued use of VAMs contributes to a belief that evaluations are not, in fact, tools to improve instruction.

That VAMs will lead to such negative results may be speculative. To be sure, the full impact of VAMs on a school culture, from an empirical sense, will not be known until they can be studied in a systematic way. However, there has been significant unrest in the education community already. The lawsuits and protests against VAMs reflect this point.

Yet notwithstanding the lack of precise empirical data on the impact of VAMs, these early signs beg the question: is the lack of empirical knowledge sufficient justification to continue the use of VAMs? If using VAMs turns out to be a poor policy decision, the damage will be immeasurable. To those on the policymaking lines, this is an academic problem.

But for those on the front lines, it is a real problem that must be reckoned with—and soon. Indeed, it appears that VAMs will continue to be part of the evaluation landscape for the foreseeable future. Their influence, then, must be managed. Aside from sweeping legislative changes,[28] this can only happen at the local level. What tools then are available to school administrators and teachers to do this?

A TWO-PRONGED LOCAL APPROACH: INTEREST-BASED COLLECTIVE BARGAINING AND PEER-ASSISTED REVIEW

This section recommends a two-pronged approach for local officials to blunt the force of VAMs on school culture. First, to the extent possible, local stakeholders should use a particular method of collective bargaining (interest-based bargaining, IBB). Second, local stakeholders should use IBB to codify a particular process of evaluating teachers (peer-assisted review, PAR). This recommendation views bargaining as an entry point through which collaboration and responsibility can be reintroduced to the school ecosystem.

Methods to Bargaining: Traditional and Interest-Based Bargaining (IBB)

There are two (2) methods for negotiating a contract: traditional bargaining and interest-based bargaining (IBB). Historically, traditional bargaining has been the method of choice. Yet, as the themes of collaboration have been promoted in education, interest-based bargaining has gained in prominence and would likely be the most effective at achieving the benefits described above. However, it is helpful to understand both means of bargaining before viewing how these methods relate to teacher evaluation policy at the local level.

Under traditional bargaining, the process is seen as adversarial. Each side—management and union—attempts to maximize the gains for its members.[29] It is a zero-sum game. Benefits that accrue to one side of the table come at the expense of the other side. The parties see bargaining as oppositional.[30] Moreover, in traditional bargaining parties cannot easily maneuver from a position; once a party publicly declares during bargaining, they feel obliged to maintain that public stance. Backing down would appear weak.

The First Prong: Interest-Based Bargaining (IBB)

In contrast, IBB views bargaining as joint problem-solving opportunity. In this context, unions and management identify the pressing issues they face together. Importantly, the touchstone question that any proposal must address is this: is the proposal in the best interests of children?

Through IBB, parties engage in "real-time" discussions over the merits of respective proposals. This contrasts from traditional bargaining, where each proposal is viewed as to the maximization of benefits for a respective side and frequently involves a caucus (i.e., each side meets privately with their own negotiating team).

Interest-based bargaining (IBB) is a well-suited method to blunt the negative forces of VAMs. The distinguishing feature of IBB is its collaborative, joint problem-solving approach; IBB requires *collaboration*. This is exactly the virtue subtracted at the local level because of VAMs.

To be sure, IBB has drawbacks. It is not always successful. It requires trust. It does not—and cannot—remove VAMs from evaluative decisions in some states. But, importantly, IBB provides a collaborative way to jointly resolve aspects of evaluation processes that the parties *do* control (e.g., what is not already spoken for under statute). The value of IBB is further enhanced if used to negotiate peer-assisted review (PAR), a particular method of evaluation.

The Second Prong: Peer-Assisted Review (PAR)

Unions and local school officials should use the IBB process to negotiate peer-assisted review (PAR) because it will further enhance collaboration.

To begin with, PARs view evaluation—and many employment decisions—as a shared endeavor. Under PAR, management and unions have considerable influence, together.

PAR systems have appealing characteristics to counteract unique problems posed by VAMs. PARs place considerable authority in the expertise of local educators. In fact, *peers* (e.g., fellow teachers) lead the evaluation and intervention processes that occur in the field. A typical PAR has a supervising teacher (herein, "ST") charged with providing assistance or evaluation. The supervising teachers, or STs, are expert teachers. They mentor new teachers and intervene with struggling veteran teachers.

PARs provide authentic instructional feedback because STs have numerous visits to classrooms, both announced and unannounced. The number of visits exceeds those performed under the typical principal-led evaluation systems. For example, one study noted that STs visited a classroom on average once a week.[31] Teachers receive prompt feedback. STs develop and apply rigorous standards to assess teaching. Thus, evaluated educators receive actionable information to improve instructional quality.

PARs involve unions and management in significant personnel decisions. Specifically, STs report on their evaluations and/or intervention efforts to a joint review board comprised of union and management personnel. Based on this, the panel makes employment recommendations (e.g., to proceed with a nonrenewal or termination). While the recommendation is nonbinding (under most state statutes, the school board makes the ultimate determination), it is worth noting the level of shared governance involved in the process.

In sum, PARs provide multiple benefits to counteract some of the collateral damage of high-stakes accountability regimens and VAMs. These include: shared governance over personnel decisions,[32] the creation and use of actionable information for instructional improvement, a cost-effective means to remove ineffective teachers, the promotion of teacher professionalization, and an increase in local control over high-stakes decisions, among others.

UNDERSTANDING PARS AND VAMs TOGETHER IN OPERATION

But the use of PARs does not remove the required use of VAMs. Because state statutes in many states require VAMs (e.g., Florida) for evaluation and high-stakes personnel decisions, VAMs will continue to be a force with which to be reckoned. Yet, here too, PARs can provide some relief. Specifically, PARs can prevent the use of VAMs in an arbitrary and capricious manner.

A hypothetical example illustrates this point. Let's assume that a VAM rating identifies an allegedly "poor performing teacher." Let's also assume that this VAM rating is in a jurisdiction that requires VAMs to be used for a substantial portion of the teacher's rating and personnel decision (e.g., Florida).

Further assume that the district has a PAR system negotiated by the union and school district. Under this system, the teacher likely would be "flagged" as needing improvement because of the VAM rating. Accordingly, a peer, expert teacher would be called in to mentor and intervene. Thus, professional judgment would be required to continue the evaluation and assessment of the teacher.

In this scenario, a supervisory teacher (ST) would have the opportunity to work for an extended period with the teacher, perhaps as much as one academic year. He or she could then account for all the factors that VAMs may not necessarily note. These include: the practices that are occurring in the class, various needs of the students (e.g., is there a disproportionate number of high-needs students or an intangible class dynamic based on student personality clashes), and other circumstances. More importantly, the ST could provide instructional feedback based on known standards and, consequently, provide an opportunity to impact the classroom instruction.

Let's assume, further, that the ST arrives at a different conclusion than the VAM ratings. In other words, the ST determines that the teacher, based on the standards and observations, is engaging in best practices, notwithstanding the poor performance of particular students. The ST provides conflicting evidence to the VAM rating. Thus, a PAR review board could discount that VAM rating.[33]

In the face of the opposing information, it would be difficult for the PAR board to recommend termination or punitive measures. To do so, would open the board to a claim that their decision was, arguably, arbitrary and capricious. That is the standard a court could apply to overturn a termination decision, in most cases. Thus, in this way, the PAR process provides a degree of insulation to a teacher (and to the district) from overly (and incorrectly) relying on a VAM rating.

WHY IBB *AND* PAR?

To be sure, PAR is not required for a school district to veto a VAM rating or to attempt to create a joint evaluation system. This could be done without formalizing PAR. Moreover, there is no need, technically, to negotiate PAR through collective bargaining. But, as noted, PAR has considerable benefit over a less informal process. It provides an accepted process. It involves professional expertise. It also has been largely accepted as an effective means to improve instructional quality, which is, after all, the ultimate goal of any evaluation system.

However, because collective bargaining provides workplace certainty and clear expectations, it promotes stability. This is important, especially in light of the political nature of local education politics and the changing nature of school boards. For example, a new school board slate may be elected and demand a top-down approach to evaluation, vesting exclusive power in the principal or superintendent. Because bargaining gives PARs the force of law, it cannot be ignored or subverted due to political ideologies.

Mitigating VAMs in States Where Bargaining Is Illegal

The discussion, thus far, relates only to states where collective bargaining is legal and where the subject of teacher evaluation is negotiable. Yet, several states prohibit bargaining or negotiations concerning teacher evaluation.[34] In these cases, school administrators and boards have more discretion for unilateral implementation. They cannot—and may not want to—engage in bargaining.

But, even where bargaining is not permitted, local school administrators can still work collaboratively. Generally speaking, nothing prohibits school administrations from exercising their discretion to use a PAR system. School districts can form working groups, comprised of teachers' representatives, to establish the parameters and authority of PARs with respect to evaluations. Moreover, in many states, administrators and unions can "meet and confer" regarding important decisions or policy changes.

To be sure, there are drawbacks in states without bargaining. Again, no requirement exists for school districts to institute PAR or work with teachers. They could exercise their authority unilaterally in almost any manner they wish. Moreover, there is no legally binding document—like the collective bargaining agreement—that can be enforced by either side. But, setting aside these issues, PAR still represents a possibility for districts operating without the benefits of mandated collective bargaining of teacher evaluation.

KEY POINTS

- Because of the top-down approach of policymakers, local school officials must develop local solutions to mitigate the negative impacts of VAMs on school culture.
- This chapter suggests that collective bargaining may be a legal structure to help remediate the negative impact of VAMs on school culture and teacher quality.
- Local administrators should consider implementing a two-pronged approach in this regard. First, education stakeholders should strongly consider using an interest-based bargaining (IBB) method to bargain. IBB is a collaborative, joint problem-solving negotiating process. Second, they should use IBB to ensure that peer-assisted review (PAR) is implemented as a means to evaluate teachers. PAR, like IBB, requires collaboration. It also involves both unions and teachers in designing fair evaluation systems and, when necessary, high-stakes employment decisions.
- The recommendations presented here are imperfect and insufficient. Because state statutes and mandates continue to require certain components of evaluations (i.e., VAMs), the use of VAMs is unavoidable. Until those barriers are removed, local stakeholders are constrained by the law of evaluation as it is specified in their particular state.

- The two-pronged approach here, however, represents the first solution proposed to equip local educators with the tools to blunt the negative force of VAMs.

NOTES

1. Emma Brown, "Nine Atlanta Educators in Test-cheating Case are Sentenced to Prison, *Washington Post,* April 14, 2015, accessed October 1, 2015, www.washingtonpost.com/local/education/eight-atlanta-educators-in-test-cheating-case-sentenced-to-prison/2015/04/14/08a9d26e-e2bc-11e4-b510-962fcfabc310_story.html.

2. The superintendent was also sentenced. Ibid.

3. Brown, supra, note 1.

4. See, for example, "Suspect Test Scores Found Across Ohio Schools," *Springfield News-Sun,* March 24, 2012, accessed November 1, 2015, www.springfieldnewssun.com/news/news/local/suspect-test-scores-found-across-ohio-schools-1/nMzYG/.

5. Government Accountability Office, "Testing Integrity Symposium: Issues and Recommendations for Best Practice," U.S. Department of Education, Institute of Education Sciences, National Center for Education Statistics (2013), accessed November 2, 2015, http://nces.ed.gov/pubs2013/2013454.pdf.

6. See, generally, Sharon L. Nichols and David Berliner, *Collateral Damage: How High-Stakes Testing Corrupts America's Schools* (Cambridge, MA: Harvard Education Press, 2010).

7. See Brown, supra, note 1.

8. Diane Ravitch, *The Death and Life of the Great American School System* (New York: Basic Books, 2011), 154. Ravitch also noted the nebulous boundary between unethical and illegal behavior, writing that: "Many ways of gaming the system are not outright illegal, yet they are usually not openly acknowledged." Ravitch at 155.

9. See, generally, Terrence Deal and Kent Peterson, *Shaping School Culture: Pitfalls, Paradoxes, and Promises* (San Francisco: Jossey Bass, 2009) for a discussion about school culture.

10. As discussed earlier, bargaining is not available to all stakeholders. However, even where bargaining is illegal, administrators can—and should—"meet and confer" with appropriate employee representatives when developing significant decisions, like teacher evaluation processes and implications.

11. To be clear: until the policy direction reverses course, it will be very difficult for this to be achieved in any true sense of the matter. The unfortunate

reality is that educators at the local level must manage the situation to the extent possible. Thus, the remedies suggested here are imperfect, incomplete solutions.

12. See Deal and Peterson, supra, note 9.

13. Ibid. at 1.

14. See Deal and Peterson, supra, note 9, 12–13. These conclusions are supported by ample reference to numerous studies. Moreover, the studies span several years, thus indicating the staying power of these conclusions. As discussed in the pages below, literature linking student outcomes and culture continues to substantiate these central points.

15. See, for example, Judith Little, "Norms of Collegiality and Experimentation: Workplace Conditions of School Success," *American Educational Research Journal* 19, no. 3 (1982): 325–340; Elizabeth Stearns, Neena Banerjee, Stephanie Moller, and Roslyn Arlin Mickelson, "Collective Pedagogical Teacher Culture and Teacher Satisfaction," *Teachers College Record* 117, no. 8 (2015): 17–18.

16. See Nicole S. Simon and Susan Moore Johnson, "Teacher Turnover in High-Poverty Schools: What We Know and Can Do," *Teacher College Record* 117, no. 3 (2015): 1.

17. The literature on PLCs is almost undisputed. See, for example, Milbrey W. McLaughlin and Joan E. Talbot, *Building School-Based Teacher Learning Communities* (New York: Teachers College Press, 2006).

18. Matthew A. Kraft and Jonathan P. Papay, "Can Professional Environments in Schools Promote Teacher Development? Explaining Heterogeneity in Returns to Teaching Experience," *Educational Evaluation and Policy Analysis* 36, no. 4 (2013): 476–500: 480.

19. Caryn M. Wells and Lindson Feun, "Educational Change and Professional Learning Communities: A Study of Two Districts," *Journal of Educational Change* 14, no. 2 (May 2013): 233–257.

20. K. S. Louis and S. D. Kruse, *Professionalism and Community: Perspectives on Reforming Urban Schools* (Thousand Oaks, CA: Corwin Press, 1995).

21. Richard Dufour and Robert Eaker, *Professional Learning Communities at Work: Best Practices for Enhancing Student Achievement* (Bloomington, IN: Solution Tree, 1998).

22. See Wells and Feun, note 19, at 236.

23. Ibid., 236.

24. See, e.g., Shirley M. Hord and William A. Sommers, *Leading Professional Learning Communities: Voices from Research and Practice* (Thousand Oaks, CA: Corwin Press, 2008).

25. See, generally, Ravitch, supra, note 8.

26. Susan Moore Johnson, "Will VAMs Reinforce the Walls of the Egg-Crate School?" *Educational Researcher* 44, no. 2 (March 2015): 117–126: 121.

27. See, generally, Richard Rothstein, *Grading Education: Getting Accountability Right* (New York: Teachers College Press, 2008).

28. This is a subject that chapter 7 addresses in considering longer-term remedial measures to halt VAMs in evaluation and employment decisions.

29. See, generally, Roger Fisher and Scott Brown, *Getting Together: Building Relationships as We Negotiate* (New York: Penguin Books, 1988).

30. Ibid.

31. Jennifer Goldstein, "Easy to Dance To: Solving the Problems of Teacher Evaluation with Peer Assistance and Review," *American Journal of Education* 113, no. 3 (May 2007): 479–508.

32. Ibid.

33. Or, in the alternative, the ST could substantiate the VAM rating.

34. North Carolina prohibits bargaining. Similarly, while bargaining is technically still permitted in Wisconsin, negotiation over teacher evaluation is prohibited.

7

THE ROLE OF COURTS IN IMPROVING TEACHER QUALITY THROUGH EVALUATION

> Neither judicial activism nor judicial restraint can be supported by an examination of the attributes of only one institution—by single institutionalism.
> —Neil Komesar, University of Wisconsin, School of Law [1]

The prior chapter outlined short-term solutions for school administrators—such as interest-based bargaining and peer-assisted review—to mitigate unintended consequences of VAMs. It emphasized collaboration with stakeholders as central to these efforts. But this is only a partial remedy. If policymakers continue to require the use of VAMs in evaluation and, more importantly, high-stakes decisions, problems will persist.

A search for longer-term remedies, therefore, is required. How can the use of VAMs be removed in evaluative decisions with employment consequences?[2] In addressing this issue, those seeking to minimize VAMs and promote alternatives must consider *where* to focus their efforts. Put another way: in which institutions—courts or legislatures—should the focus be? Reforming the current evaluation reforms presents a question of institutional choice.

The chapter explores these questions. It employs a *comparative institutional analysis*.[3] Comparative institutional analysis assesses the capacity of available institutions (courts, legislatures, or markets) to remedy a public policy or legal concern. Once this is ascertained, practitioners and policymakers can efficiently direct resources toward a solution.

The chapter concludes that stakeholders and policy-reformers should primarily focus on political institutions (rather than courts) to alter VAM-based laws. Courts hesitate to sort through the difficult policy issues raised in VAM-based litigation. In contrast, the political process offers opportunities for interest groups—such as teachers, administrators, and parents—to pressure for immediate legislative action.

Unfortunately, education researchers seeking to reverse the curse of VAMs have invested hope, too much hope, in court action. One education professor stated as follows:

> As I have written and said before, I believe the VAM-related "wars" will be won out in the courthouse. Hopefully this, as well as some of the other key lawsuits currently underway in these other states . . . will continue to take the lead, and *even lead our nation* back to a more reasonable and valid set of standards and expectations when it comes to the evaluation of America's public school teachers. Do stay tuned. (emphasis added)[4]

But the faith in a court remedy to the problems created by VAMs may be misplaced, as the *Cook v. Stewart* case from Florida reminds us. This significant decision makes clear that the battle over VAMs *will likely not* be won in the courts, especially at the federal level. In fact, continued pursuit of a legal remedy—without primary attention to seeking a remedy through political institutions—will prolong the use of VAMs.

This chapter outlines comparative institutional analysis. It then discusses the relative capacity of courts and legislatures with respect to resolving education law and policy disputes, such as those presented by the use of VAMs in the law. Second, the chapter highlights the case of Florida. In that state, political pressure has blunted the advancement of VAM-based evaluation policies.

SEEKING A SOLUTION: COMPARATIVE INSTITUTIONAL ANALYSIS

Understanding how to resolve unintended consequences created by VAM-based evaluation statutes requires a *comparative institutional anal-*

ysis. This framework assesses the relative capacity of available institutions (courts, political processes) to remedy a set particular policy and legal issues.[5]

In brief, all policymaking institutions have relative strengths and weaknesses. These, in turn, must be assessed against the particular problem at hand to best understand which of these institutions is the most appropriate forum to achieve a desired result. In the context of VAMs, then, which, among the institutional choices, is best equipped to modify our current use of VAMs? We choose "the best of bad alternatives."[6] The answer to the question, in the end, is one of "imperfect alternatives."[7]

The Law's Limits: The Role of Courts in Education Law and Policy

Typically, courts avoid education policy matters that present in the context of litigation. There are several reasons for this general avoidance. First, courts recognize a separation of powers between the branches of government. Voters elect legislators to make certain policy decisions on their behalf. Courts, as a general rule, cannot overturn these policy choices, unless they cross constitutional or statutory limits. If a case centers primarily on policy choices, courts sparingly intervene. Policy change occurs, therefore, at the ballot.

Second, and in a related point, courts have consistently deferred to local and state officials on school management and direction, including issues related to the use of standardized tests.[8] In *Debra P. v. Turlington*, for instance, a federal court of appeals upheld a state testing system whereby students' high school diplomas were linked to scores on state standardized tests.[9]

Third, judges and courts lack technical expertise in education and statistical matters. Asking courts to decide issues that are highly technical in nature requires them to engage in a level of analysis outside their own expertise. This is important in considering VAM-based litigation. To be sure, they may have some abilities in this regard. But their primary training, experience, and abilities are legal in nature. Cases thus far have created something of a battle of the experts and, in such situations, may make courts hesitant to engage.

Fourth, courts have difficulty fashioning remedies, particularly with respect to education policy issues. If a court strikes down a particular law, the question then arises: what is the appropriate change or remedy needed to rectify the wrong? Again, in many instances, courts are powerless to fashion what may be the appropriate remedy. For instance, if a court found a school finance system unconstitutional because of lack of resources, it cannot order the necessary remedy: increased revenue. Raising and appropriating is a legislative function. Similarly, even if a court strikes down VAM mandates, the legislature must tailor an evaluation system that ensures teacher quality.

Fifth, substantial court precedence exists that limits court involvement on questions of VAMs. Again, it is worth noting that the case of *Cook v. Stewart* illustrates this point. That case effectively inoculates Florida's VAM-based evaluation processes from challenges arising under constitutional law. Federal courts have been effectively limited as a means for challenges to similar evaluation systems nationwide.[10]

Representative Examples: Courts and High-Stakes Testing Policy Litigation

It is helpful to examine several cases that demonstrate the limits of courts with respect to altering education policy judgments, especially in situations related to high-stakes testing. While the cases do not relate to challenges involving employment decisions related to teacher evaluation per se (with the exception of *Cook v. Florida*), they do involve challenges related to the legality of using high-stakes testing in education policy (e.g., requiring that students pass a specific standardized exam to meet graduation requirements).

Pontiac v. Secretary of Education and *Connecticut v. Duncan*

In *Pontiac v. Secretary of Education* several school districts and education associations asked a federal court to issue a declaratory judgment regarding the constitutionality of No Child Left Behind.[11] In brief, the plaintiffs contended that the accountability requirements under NCLB (e.g., high-stakes testing) unconstitutionally required local districts to expend their own funds on a federal mandate. According to the plaintiffs, this violated the Unfunded Mandates Provision of NCLB, and therefore, rendered the testing requirements unconstitutional.[12]

The federal sixth circuit court of appeals rejected the plaintiffs' claims. To be fair, the court did not rest its conclusion on policy grounds, per se. In other words, its ruling in favor of the government was not predicated on the notion that the issue was, fundamentally, a policy dispute and, therefore, more appropriately decided through the political process. However, it is undeniable that the case represents at least one point where courts declined to interfere with a statutory structure based on high-stakes accountability.

In *Connecticut v. Duncan,* the second circuit court of appeals reached a conclusion similar to that in the *Pontiac* decision.[13] In *Duncan*, the state of Connecticut claimed that the costs associated with implementing the testing requirements under NCLB exceeded the amount of the federal funds delivered to the state. Yet, like the sixth circuit, the *Duncan* court refused to find a constitutional violation.

The second circuit court of appeals' ruling affirmed a lower court ruling. The lower court's reasoning is significant for purposes of understanding the institutional hesitation of courts to engage in adjudicating some fundamental policy disputes. Indeed, the district court noted a guiding principle of its decision and wrote:

> Finally, courts have wisely developed important prudential rules to ensure that they exercise restraint and do not unnecessarily inject themselves into disputes committed to the other branches of Government or before the time at which judicial action is required.[14]

Without question the district court (and the appellate court that largely affirmed the decision) are quite aware of the politically charged nature of the issue and the need to preserve institutional territory. The district court pointed this out[15] and noted that restrictions on judicial authority recognized that for a democracy to function properly, courts must be restrained.[16]

Other scholars have noted the courts' reluctance with respect to involvement related to overturning legislative actions using high-stakes testing. For example, one commentator, after surveying several other cases wherein courts refused to overturn the legislative action, summarized the situation as follows:

> The trend of several decades of litigation aimed at disrupting high-stakes testing policies suggests that judges are becoming hesitant to

second-guess policymakers who carefully design and implement high-stakes tests.[17]

This line of logic—that the courts are not the appropriate institution to determine major policy issues—has been explicitly adopted in challenges to VAM-based decisions.[18] And this makes sense in many cases involving education policy disputes. A researcher has succinctly noted that "[t]he outcomes of education litigation often work better in the courtroom than in the classroom or the principal's office."[19] Put slightly differently, court-ordered education policy can have a negative impact on the daily operation of a school, notwithstanding courts' best intentions.

In sum, the cases above reflect a general judicial reluctance to overrule education policy actions based on high-stakes testing—even if it is unwise. Barring discriminatory motives or impact, they will not rule against policy judgments that heavily rely on standardized tests such as VAMs.

What Is the Role of Courts in High-Stakes Policy Debate?

Yet courts *do* play an important role in the overall debate concerning high-stakes testing in education policy. Indeed, litigation—or the threat of litigation—can add a number of assets to an overall effort to change policies through the political process. In surveying the impact of litigation involving challenges to high-stakes testing regimens (with the exception of VAMs), one scholar has noted the following:

> Litigation (and its threat) led to many changes in test policies—including delayed implementation, increased resources for students who struggle with such tests, and more forgiving pass rates—all of which reveal policymakers' increased sensitivity to legal exposure.[20]

In other words, litigation can have a lasting impact, if used in coordination with other efforts.

A number of attributes and the value of litigation in this regard deserve mention. For instance, litigation can call attention to an issue. Indeed, many of the court challenges to VAMs (and other high-stakes testing) produce substantive conversations in policy circles. At the very least, the attention puts a spotlight on the issue, sometimes in the media. This effect can be particularly impactful in today's age of technology where information passes so freely and frequently; a legal challenge to a hot-button issue will most certainly capture some attention.

Litigation can foster compromise. When facing a lawsuit, both parties scrutinize their relative positions for strengths and weaknesses. In recognizing these relative positions, a party may be more willing to compromise or change their opinion in light of this assessment. Similarly, because litigation can be expensive, both parties may be incentivized to seek middle ground.

Litigation also causes delay of a full policy implementation. Years can pass between the filing of a lawsuit and its ultimate resolution through the courts. Thus, in this regard, litigation can buy time for advocates to strategize and lobby the political branch to change their course of action, or at least address particular weaknesses in an education policy, such as the use of VAMs in high-stakes testing. This is exactly what has occurred—and likely will continue to occur—in Florida, as discussed below.

The Political Process and Education Law and Policy

Comparative institutional analysis requires us to look at the issue of teacher evaluation, VAMs, and the law with reference to the legislature and political process. If courts are not particularly well positioned to solely address the issues associated with VAMs (as outlined here), then we must also understand how the political process can contribute to this effort.

At first blush, the notion of using the political process seems counterintuitive. Politics is almost a "four-letter word" in the American dialect. But the political process is subject to pressure from grassroots and interest groups, unlike the courts (in theory). Moreover, state legislatures *created* the statutory framework mandating VAMs and, therefore, seem like the logical—and most efficient—place to reverse or amend those statutes.

Initial indications suggest that the political process can provide a successful avenue to reform misguided evaluation laws that rely on high-stakes testing. Across the country parents, teachers' groups, administrators, and other interest groups have publicly protested the overreliance on tests in public education. The government—the political process—appears to be listening. State legislatures have reduced the proportion of evaluations based on VAMs and their link to high-stakes decisions. The case of Florida, discussed below, is significant in this regard.

Florida: Rolling Back VAMs

Recent events in Florida illustrate the respective roles that legislatures and courts can play in reforming the use of VAMs in high-stakes employment matters. In that state, as noted, legal challenges were unsuccessful. Yet, the Florida state legislature recently amended its evaluation statutes to reduce the level of reliance on VAMs for high-stakes purposes.

VAMs in Florida: A Brief History

In 2011, the Florida state legislature significantly amended teacher evaluation and employment statutes with the passage of Senate Bill 736 (SB 736). Significantly, SB 736, as passed, required that a teacher's evaluation be based in substantial part ("at least 50 percent") on student performance on state standardized tests. It linked a teacher's compensation and continued employment status to the resulting evaluation.

The change engendered controversy. The state's teachers unions opposed the changes. But Florida's governor Rick Scott stood firm. For example, in his state of the state address on March 8, 2011, Scott stated as follows:

> [W]e can all agree that measuring results is a key aspect of education. We must test our students, and we must evaluate our educators. Those measurements need to be fair and thoughtful, *and they need to have rewards and consequences.* (emphasis supplied).[21]

Several days following this remark, he signed into law SB 736.[22]

In 2013, Scott reiterated his stance on the changes. Regarding the changes through SB 736, he noted as follows: "[T]hanks to our work, we are now in a better position than ever before to reward good teachers and move bad teachers out of the classroom."[23]

Cook v. Stewart: Seeking Court Remedy to SB 736 and VAMs

Opponents to SB 736 brought their claims to federal district court in the case of *Cook v. Stewart*. Specifically, plaintiffs argued that the changes under SB 736 violated the federal constitution.[24] They documented statistical flaws inherent in the VAM-based evaluations. They noted that a system that ranked teachers based on test scores of students that they never instructed was irrational and therefore unconstitutional.

The court was sympathetic to the plaintiff-teachers' arguments but, importantly, it did not find a constitutional violation. It upheld the evaluation system, but noted that it seemed unfair. The eleventh circuit court of appeals affirmed that decision, leaving the evaluation system completely intact, as discussed in prior chapters.[25]

Legislative Amendments to SB 736: A Political Response

Yet, the *Cook* decision may have helped trigger political movement to change the evaluation system. Indeed, since *Cook,* the Florida legislature has made significant changes in their use of VAMs in teacher evaluation. These, in general, have diluted the impact of VAMs on a teacher evaluation. To be sure, student achievement on standardized tests continues to be a factor. But, importantly, the legislature has amended its statutory evaluation scheme in important ways so as to reduce this emphasis.

For example, in 2013, the legislature passed—and Governor Scott signed—SB 1664, "An act to relating to the repeal of education provisions."[26] The act repealed the requirement that teachers be evaluated based on test scores of students they never instructed. This was primary issue contested in *Cook*. Thus, arguably, the *Cook* decision (and the media attention the lawsuit generated) forced the legislature to deal with the flaws of the policy.

In addition, the Florida legislature reduced the percentage of evaluations based on VAMs. Specifically, on April 14, 2014, Florida governor Rick Scott signed into law House Bill 7069 (HB 7069) which took effect immediately. Under the amended statute, "at least 1/3" of an evaluation must be based on student performance (including, where applicable, performance as rated by the state's growth model). Prior law required that "at least 50 percent" of an evaluation be based upon student performance.

State legislative leaders in Florida were blunt in their assessment that the state government had overreached with respect to the evaluation policy. The State Senate Education Committee Chairman, John Legg, commented as follows: "We were trying to prove a point, and we became overprescriptive."[27] He further noted that, in the face of district resistance, the legislature "can scale back."[28]

The political changes, arguably, occurred because of efforts first undertaken in the courts.[29] Political interest groups, rightfully, took credit for forcing the legislature to change. Significantly, many linked this political success to their court-driven efforts at reform. The state's National Education Association (NEA) affiliate, as well, attributed the legislative changes to court action. Following the legislative changes, its website proclaimed that "Teachers Lawsuit Leads to Reboot by Florida Legislature."[30]

The composition of the interest groups opposed to the use of VAMs spanned a wide spectrum. In addition to teachers' unions, school administrators lobbied against the continued emphasis on VAMs. For example, the Florida Association of District School Superintendents (FADSS) took a position to reduce the amount of student performance used in an evaluation in 2014.[31] The FADSS also demanded more local flexibility, especially with respect to how pay would be linked to performance.

Parent interest groups joined the opposition to standardized testing. Numerous "opt-out" groups emerged in the state to protest the legislature's continued reliance and promotion of standardized tests.[32] The parents' reaction caught the attention of state lawmakers.[33] While the opt-out movement is tangentially linked to teacher evaluations using VAMs, they reflect a public mood vis-à-vis high-stakes testing and accountability.

Florida is just one example of how the political process and court action can operate to reverse or stymy poor evaluation policies. A very similar situation occurred in Tennessee. In that state, the teachers union challenged the VAM-based evaluation system in federal courts. Like the *Cook* case in Florida, teachers did not prevail.

Yet, the Tennessee legislature scaled back their use of VAMs in evaluation. Specifically, it reduced the portion of an evaluation based on student growth measures. It also disconnected the link between evaluations and tenure. Thus, similar to the Florida situation, court involvement called attention to the unfairness of the system and, in the process, refocused efforts to change the policy through the political process.

In New York, political institutions are reducing the use of student test scores in teacher evaluation. Like the case in Florida, New York governor Andrew Cuomo was a strong advocate of the use of standardized tests and teacher evaluation. Yet, it has been reported that the governor has quietly reversed that stance and sought to reduce the link between test scores and evaluations.[34]

Congressional Action: Every Student Succeeds Act

The recently passed the Every Student Succeeds Act (ESSA) illustrates the impact of the federal political process on reducing the use of test scores in evaluation. As you may recall, federal action through the Race to the Top Fund triggered the incorporation of test scores as a means to evaluate teachers. However, Congress reversed course (partially) with its passage of the ESSA. In particular, state and local education agencies are not required to use student test scores in teacher evaluations.[35]

The rollback of federal involvement in education policy—particularly as it relates to the use of high-stakes testing—is a remarkable change of events. Indeed, with the Race to the Top initiative of 2008, the federal government explicitly conditioned the receipt of federal funds, as noted. Yet, with the 2015 ESSA, that requirement has been completely removed.

KEY POINTS

- Evaluation laws and policies that rely on VAMs must be amended to reduce their reliance on standardized tests.
- There are two institutions through which such changes can occur. These are courts and political processes. Both courts and the political processes have relative strengths and weaknesses that must be considered.
- Courts typically avoid questions that appear to be primarily related to matters of education policy. Based on principles of separation of powers, these issues are more properly addressed through the political processes.
- Court action will not, alone, resolve the fairness issues that have been raised by VAMs. However, court action can be part of a larger strategy to amend evaluation laws.

- Political institutions may be responsive to pleas to change current evaluation laws that rely heavily on test scores.
- There are early indications that legislatures recognize that an overly prescriptive evaluation system based on standardized test scores linked to personnel decisions may be misguided. In Florida, for example, the legislature and governor have reduced their reliance on test scores for evaluation and personnel purposes.
- Similarly, the federal government has minimized its role in requiring the use of VAMs with the recent passage of the Every Student Succeeds Act.
- Overall, responses that have resulted in reducing the use of VAMs may have been triggered by court action. On questions of policy and law, "institutions tend to move together."[36] Thus, as courts shine light on unfair (but not unconstitutional) evaluation mechanisms, legislatures cannot simply ignore those facts.

NOTES

1. Neil K. Komesar, *Law's Limits: The Rule of Law and the Supply and Demand of Rights* (New York: Cambridge University Press, 2001), 176.
2. Again, it is worth noting that the book does not take the position that VAMs have no place in education. They may have some value, and this is a question for another day. But it has become clear that their statistical flaws are not improving teacher quality and, in fact, are causing more frustration to local efforts in this regard.
3. See, Komesar, *Law's Limits*, supra, note 1.
4. Audrey Amrein-Beardsley, "Lawsuit in New Mexico Challenging State's Teacher Evaluation System," February 15, 2015, accessed October 21, 2015, http://vamboozled.com/lawsuit-in-new-mexico-challenging-states-teacher-evaluation-system/.
5. Markets are another available institution. However, they are irrelevant to this particular issue.
6. Ibid., 24.
7. Ibid.
8. See, for example, *Wisconsin v. Yoder*, 406 U.S. 205 (1972).
9. *Debra P. v. Turlington*, 644 F.2d 397 (5th Cir. 1981).
10. To be sure, sister appellate courts are not bound by this appellate court. However, it should be noted that the court's opinion does have weight in all

federal courts. It is, at least, persuasive to other appellate courts. And it will certainly have to be addressed in any federal litigation as a legal authority.

11. *Pontiac v. Secretary of Education,* 584 F.3d 253 (6th Cir. 2009).

12. The claim arose under the Constitution's Spending Clause. That clause requires that when Congress imposes conditions or requirements on acceptance of a grant, such as funds coming under NCLB, it must clearly express its intent so that the states understand what is required and whether to accept those funds. See, generally, *Pennhurst State School and Hospital v. Halderman,* 451 U.S. 1 (1981).

13. *Connecticut v. Duncan,* 612 F.3d 107 (2d Cir. 2010).

14. *Connecticut v. Spellings,* 453 F. Supp. 2d 459, 465 (D. Conn. 2006); affirmed as modified sub nom., *Connecticut v. Duncan,* 612 F.3d 107 (2d Cir. 2010).

15. Michael Heise, "Pass or Fail? Litigating High-Stakes Testing," in *From Schoolhouse to Courthouse: The Judiciary's Role in American Education*, ed. Joshua Dunn and Martin R. West (Washington, DC: Brookings Institution, 2009): 142–163: 155.

16. *Connecticut v. Spellings,* supra, note 14, at 465.

17. Heise, supra, note 15, at 155.

18. To be sure, court involvement in education policy (outside of cases involving high-stakes testing) is quite frequent. This has been particularly apparent in state school finance litigation. In this context, challenges have met a favorable audience in state courts. The majority of state courts that have heard school finance challenges have ruled that the system is unconstitutional. Yet, at the same time, the capacity of courts is taxed in the remedial phase of a trial (i.e., where the court must order and oversee a remedy to the cause of the problem). In the case of school finance litigation, the disputes, at bottom, involve issues of resource allocation and distribution (taxing and spending) which are squarely in the domain of the legislature. For an excellent overview of the role of courts in school finance, see Michael A. Rebell, *Courts and Kids: Pursuing Educational Equity through the State Courts* (Chicago: University of Chicago Press, 2011), note 9.

19. Chester Finn, "Foreword," in *From Schoolhouse to Courthouse: the Judiciary's Role in American Education*, ed. Joshua Dunn and Martin West (Washington, DC: Brookings Institution, 2009): ix–xii: ix.

20. Ibid. at 149.

21. "Florida Governor Rick Scott Delivers State of the State Address," accessed April 5, 2016, www.flgov.com/2011/03/08/florida-governor-rick-scott-delivers-state-of-the-state-address/.

22. Aaron Sharockman, "Rick Scott's first bill signing moves Scott-o-meter," Politifact, March 24, 2011, accessed April 5, 2015, www.politifact.com/florida/article/2011/mar/24/rick-scotts-first-bill-signing-moves-Scott-o-meter.

23. Gina Jordan, "Governor: 'We Don't Want A War On Teachers; We Want A War On Failure,'" Florida: Putting Education Reform to the Test, *State Impact*, March 5, 2013, accessed April 11, 2015, https://stateimpact.npr.org/florida/2013/03/05/governor-we-dont-want-a-war-on-teachers-we-want-a-war-on-failure/.

24. A more thorough discussion of *Cook v. Stewart* can be found in chapter 3.

25. Ibid.

26. Office of Governor Rick Scott, "Governor Scott signs 60 bills into law today," accessed April 5, 2015, www.flgov.com/governor-scott-signs-60-bills-into-law-today-2/.

27. Jeffrey Solochek, "Teachers Remain Wary Even as Florida Eases its Stance on Evaluations," *Tampa Bay Times*, June 13, 2015, accessed April 11, 2015, www.tampabay.com/news/education/teachers/teachers-remain-wary-even-as-florida-eases-its-stance-on-teacher/2233572, accessed November 2, 2015.

28. Ibid.

29. Broward Teachers' Union AFT Local 1975, *BTU Membership Update*, Special Summer Edition, 2013.

30. Florida Education Association, "Teachers' Lawsuit Leads to Reboot by Florida Legislature: Governor Rick Scott Signs Partial Fix for Flawed Teacher Evaluation System," accessed November 9, 2015, https://feaweb.org/teachers-lawsuit-leads-to-reboot-by-florida-legislature.

31. Florida Association of District School Superintendents, "2014 Legislative Platform," 4.

32. See Kathleen McGrory, "Parents Push Back on Florida's Standardized Testing System," *Miami Herald*, September 26, 2015, accessed November 5, 2015, www.miamiherald.com/news/local/education/article2261678.html.

33. Ibid.

34. Kate Taylor, "Cuomo, in Shift, Is Said to Back Reducing Test Scores in Teacher Reviews," *The New York Times*, November 25, 2015, accessed December 29, 2015, www.nytimes.com/2015/11/26/nyregion/cuomo-in-shift-is-said-to-back-reducing-test-scores-role-in-teacher-reviews.html?_r=0.

35. Public Law 114–95, S.1177, *Every Student Succeeds Act* (ESSA).

36. Komesar, *Law's Limits*, 24.

8

LESSONS LEARNED

What Policymakers Can Learn from Education Professionals

Reflection is a good thing. In order to avoid errors, or improve our performance, we must consider our past actions and learn from them. In teaching and learning, reflection is necessary to improve instruction and, in the end, increase student success. In education, we want all teachers—even those we deem as masters in the profession—to be improving. Master teachers are master teachers because of a reflective tendency. They understand that teaching is part art and part science and, therefore, are constantly tinkering toward improvement.

Education policymakers might learn something from the education profession with respect to reflection. Indeed, those imposing policy reforms must adopt a more reflective practice, such as that demonstrated by master teachers. This is especially true in cases where policies have such high stakes, like teacher evaluation and employment.

There is always an attraction to "bright and shiny objects" in education policy. VAM-based evaluation systems are today's educational flavor of the week, the new panacea. Wrapped in complicated statistical models, they are hard to resist. Yet the time has come to seriously consider the repercussions of imposing these models with an almost reckless abandon.

Thus, the remaining portion of this book is reflective in nature. It seeks to take the lessons we have learned from VAMs and put them to the page, for future reference. They are in no particular order. It is not an exhaustive list by any means. Readers may list numerous other lessons from the natural experiment of VAMs. The lessons learned simply are points for continued discussion.

LESSONS LEARNED

There are significant costs in using the law to advance questionable policies.

The implementation of VAMs—as a legal construct in evaluation systems—came with significant costs. This book catalogued numerous litigation battles that are directly linked to their use. As we know, litigation is expensive. It's long. It is, in a word, inefficient. It requires local school districts to divert resources from the classroom to the courtroom. Court action is draining.

To be sure, some things are worth litigating. But given administrator hesitation about using VAMs and the questions surrounding them, this may not be a battle worth having. Perhaps, at this point, the money being spent on litigation may be more beneficial to kids and schools. There may be some day where the statistical issues around VAMs are largely resolved and expensive legal battles justified.[1] Today, that is not the case.

Poorly designed policies applied in high-stakes situations can have psychological and institutional costs. Teaching morale is already at historic lows. Retaining teachers—especially in high-needs areas—is incredibly difficult. VAMs only exacerbate this problem because of their zero-sum-game nature. There are winners and losers. Significantly, these rules of the game are embedded in law; local administrators cannot adjust accordingly. It is difficult to see how these rules of the game will improve school culture.

It may have been more productive to *recommend rather than require* the use of VAMs. The Every Student Succeeds Act (ESSA) in federal law allows this option, to some extent. If local stakeholders believe that VAMs should be incorporated in their evaluation systems, then that is their decision (assuming the state does not mandate their use). Regardless, a recommendation, rather than a requirement, allows school districts to assess their local needs and devise policy appropriately.

LESSONS LEARNED

Business models do not always transfer to public education policy.

Education is constantly criticized because of perceived inefficiencies. We hear frequently that teacher contracts are bloated with benefits that sap employee drive or do little to advance student achievement. A common refrain, especially with respect to employment practices in education, is that such practices would never be tolerated in the private sector. Yet these refrains are often not grounded in fact.

To resolve these perceived problems, education has historically looked to the private sector. This has been the case with the accountability movement. In the current context, we frequently hear the buzzwords such as "metrics," "data-driven decision-making," and "deliverables," among other phrases that are derived from the private sector.

Understanding the relationship between inputs and outputs is a good thing, of course, in the public sector. Taxpayers deserve to understand what impact their dollars have. But measuring inaccurately leads to unintended consequences. As two commentators succinctly note:

> Measuring outcomes badly or incompletely, however, can bring risks and pitfalls of its own. Getting measurement wrong, whether because it is too narrow or too loosely connected to the outcome you really care about, can lead to disappointment or worse. This problem can be exacerbated when rewards or punishments are connected to performance on the measures you are using.[2]

Thus, the carpenter's adage "measure twice, cut once" is certainly appropriate.

Moreover, the private sector is by no means efficient. The words "private sector" are not magical in their own right. We have a litany of examples of this in the private sector. These include the use of subprime lending and derivatives, among others.

In fact, recent trends among some large corporations suggest that the private sector is moving in the opposite direction of education policy with respect to evaluation. For example, General Electric (GE) one of the country's largest employers reported that the company would "kill its annual performance review."[3]

The reasons for GE's decision are particularly relevant to the discussion of VAMs. Indeed, GE (and others) note that annual reviews typically provide no actionable information. In a fast-moving, data-driven environment, an annual review provides stale information, leaving little opportunity for an employee to improve or change behavior. In addition, the annual review—and its connection to pay and standing in the company—undercuts employee morale and worker allegiance to the company. In sum, annual and high-stakes reviews alienate employees, erroneously assume what motivates employees, detract from worker satisfaction, and provide no actionable feedback.

Education policymakers should take note of GE's shift. The business community appears to be moving in precisely the *opposite* direction of education evaluation. Indeed, the for-profit industries—those that are frequently heralded as models for public schools—appear to be softening the implications of performance evaluations as they relate to employment decisions.

The federal government is too involved in education, and this burdens local education agencies.

The use of VAMs in evaluation and high-stakes employment decisions raises another flag with respect to the role of the federal government in education. As noted in earlier chapters, we can link state evaluation policy to the Race to the Top initiative. Receipt of RttT funds was predicated on making changes that required the use of VAMs in teacher evaluation.

RttT and its promotion of VAMs add to the already long list of federal laws that have increased the burdens on local school districts. Others include the Individuals with Disabilities Education Act (the IDEA) which requires every school district to provide a Free Appropriate Public Education (FAPE) to students with disabilities. The goals of the IDEA are right; for too long local districts neglected the needs of these students. But the IDEA, when passed, promised that local school districts would be reimbursed for approximately 67 percent of the costs associated with complying with the IDEA. That has never happened.

Similar criticisms have been leveled—and litigated—with respect to No Child Left Behind (NCLB). The previous chapter highlighted litigation involving the claim that NCLB amounted to an unfunded mandated because of the costs associated with curriculum redesign and test implementation.[4]

The recent passage of the Every Student Succeeds Act (ESSA) rolled back federal involvement. The act removes federal involvement on matters such as teacher evaluation and the use of test scores. This reduced role reflects a more balanced and proportional involvement of the federal government in public education. Federal funding amounts to approximately 10 percent of most school district budgets. Yet, until recently, the federal policy initiatives appeared to have a disproportionate amount of influence on the direction of local school districts' policies.

Allowing local leaders to determine the appropriate role of VAMs is consistent with our accepted school governance model that emphasizes local control. Local taxpayers fund the largest portion of public school budgets, in general. It seems that they should have the most discretion with respect to the use of those monies. To be sure, the federal government has an important role in ensuring and protecting civil rights. But, setting that aside, it may be time for return of power to local school boards accountable to local voters.

Local education stakeholders and interest groups need to seize the policy initiative.

Local stakeholders must step up to the plate and assume the burdens of resolving some of the thorniest policy issues. The larger question—improving teacher quality—remains. No one can claim that simply eliminating the use of VAMs solves this issue. Thus, local education stakeholders—unions and management—now "own" this issue.

The troubles of VAMs represent an opportunity for school administrators, teachers, and unions. They can seize the moment to demonstrate that they can resolve the issues we know exist in teacher evaluation. If they work together, and rigorously reflect on how to fix the system, they will improve the status of education as a profession.

In a related point, education interest groups should focus resources and attention at the statehouse rather than the courthouse. And, frequently, disparate interest groups should seek common ground. There are instances where there may be "strange bedfellows." VAMs may be one of those issues; school administrators and teachers unions share some interest in reforming or removing VAMs in evaluation. Indeed, many school administrators do not seem to have faith in VAMs, at least as they are being used for high-stakes purposes.

Education advocacy at the court level must be exercised judiciously.

Courts have played a significant role in deciding legal issues related to education policy and the law. In particular instances, they have unquestionably righted some of the worst wrongs in our country. That was the case in *Brown v. Board of Education.*[5]

But courts are cautious in exercising their jurisdiction over education cases. They avoid policy questions. They defer to school administrators and state education agencies when possible. They restrict involvement to more extreme instances—where an agency institutes a policy or regulation for discriminatory purposes, as was the case in *Brown v. Board of Education.*

But if a case presents as a "vanilla" policy dispute, courts will hesitate to involve the judicial branch. Sorting through policy choices is not in their constitutional division of labor; that's the job of the legislature.

There is no magic solution.

At the risk of being overly simplistic, this must be stated: complex problems generally require complex solutions. Yet, the parade of simple panaceas continues in education. And VAMs have particular appeal in this regard.

There are hard truths that administrators and teachers must confront with respect to teacher quality and evaluation. Effective evaluation requires hard work. It takes time. School administrators—principals and superintendents—must be committed to that work, as most are. To be sure, administrators are overwhelmed. They frequently note that there simply is not enough time in a day to meet all the demands of their jobs. But dedicating the time and commitment to evaluating teachers is not a discretionary task for administrators. It is unavoidable.

At the same time, state and federal bureaucrats can refrain from becoming overly involved in matters of local concern. Indeed, perhaps the best course of action, then, is to give administrators and educators that freedom, interfering as little as possible. More flexibility and autonomy in the education profession—not less—may actually be the first step in improving teacher quality.

NOTES

1. If this day comes, it will reduce the volume of litigation. Indeed, if VAMs are sound, teachers and unions would be less inclined to challenge them because they would stand less of a chance of succeeding on the merits.

2. Robert Reischauer and Michael McPherson, "Measure What Matters in Education," *Washington Monthly* (blog), May 15, 2013, www.washingtonmonthly.com/college_guide/feature/how_to_measure_education_outco.php, accessed November 10, 2015.

3. Max Nisen, "It's A Millennial Thing: Why GE Had to Kill Its Annual Performance Reviews after More than Three Decades," *Quartz,* August 13, 2015, accessed, November 15, 2015, http://qz.com/428813/ge-performance-review-strategy-shift/.

4. Again, it is worth pointing out that these federal laws have had a positive impact. NCLB, in the least, called attention to disparities in achievement based on race or other demographics.

5. *Brown v. Board of Education of Topeka*, 347 U.S. 483 (1954).

INDEX

accountability, high-stakes, xii, 77–78
ADA. *See* Americans with Disabilities Act
administrative law judge (ALJ), 56–57, 61n31
administrators, deference to, pre-VAM cases involving, 48–52
age, as protected class, 26, 41n12
Ahern v. King, 39–40
ALJ. *See* administrative law judge
American Statistical Association (ASA), x, 2
Americans with Disabilities Act (ADA), 81
Anoka-Hennepin school board, 49
arbitration, 64, 67–69; authority and, 68; costs for, 69; employee favoring in, 69; final and binding, 65; worker morale in, 69; worker productivity in, 69; workplace issues and, 68–69
ASA. *See* American Statistical Association
authority, arbitration and, 68

bargaining: collective, 78; illegal, VAMs mitigation in, 87–88, 91n34; mandatory subject of, 65, 66; methods to, 83–84; permissive subject of, 65, 66, 74n11; prohibited subject of, 65, 66; VAMs in, xvii. *See also* collective bargaining agreement; interest-based bargaining
Baxter, Jerry, 77
bias, 5–6, 7

Board of Education, Bellmore-Merrick Central High School District v. Bellmore-Merrick United Secondary Teachers, Inc., 71, 75n31
Braun, Henry, 5, 19–20
Brown v. Board of Education, 111–112
"business lexicon," 79

California Achievement Test (CAT), equal protection clause violation and, 28–29
CAT. *See* California Achievement Test
CBA. *See* collective bargaining agreement
classroom sorting, 6, 11n29, 12n32. *See also* randomization
collaborative frameworks, 80, 81
collective bargaining, 78; illegal, VAMs mitigation in, 87–88, 91n34; unions and, 66; VAMs in, xvii. *See also* interest-based bargaining
collective bargaining agreement (CBA), 63–64; in education, 66; scope of, 65–66; state legislature on, 65; of teacher evaluation, 66; VAMs on, 66–67, 74n14, 74n15, 74n16; workplace stability and, 64–65
comparative institutional analysis, xviii, 93, 94–95
Connecticut v. Duncan, 97–98, 105n17
Constitution, U. S.: *Cook v. Stewart*, 31, 33–34, 36, 42n25; equal protection claims, 35–36; Fourteenth Amendment,

24, 24–25; New York, 39–40; in public school origins, 46–48; substantive due process challenge, 34–35; VAMs, 31–36
Cook, Kim, 1
Cook v. Florida, 96
Cook v. Stewart, xvi–xvii, 23, 24, 31, 33–34, 36, 41n9, 42n25, 94, 96, 101, 104n10; district court (trial court) decision in, 33–34; Eleventh Circuit Court of Appeals decision, 36; SB 736 and, 101
cooperating teacher (CT), VAMs ratings and, 86–87
culture. *See* school culture
Cuomo, Andrew, 103
curricula focus, narrowing of, 81

Debra P. v. Turlington, 95
Department of Education, 39, 61n29
Dewey, Andrew, xv, xvi, xviii
DIBELS. *See* Dynamic Indicators of Basic Early Literacy Skills tests
dismissal, of teacher, x, xiiin4, 71, 85; procedural due process in, 27; standardized tests and, 45–46
due process, 47–48
Dynamic Indicators of Basic Early Literacy Skills tests (DIBELS), 56

education: CBA in, 66; federal government involvement in, 110–111, 113n4
education advocacy, at court level, 111–112
education law and policy: courts role in, 95–96, 104n10, 105n17; reflection and, 107–108
Eleventh Circuit Court of Appeals decision, *Cook v. Stewart*, 36
employment: arbitration in, 69–70; individualized test scores and, 24, 37, 41n7; negotiation, school boards in, 64; teacher evaluation systems in, 19; VAMs in, x–xi, 45, 93, 104n2
equal protection clause, 35–36, 42n40; CAT and, 28–29; federal constitutional cases and, 35–36; of Fourteenth Amendment, 25–26

Every Student Succeeds Act (ESSA), xix, 103, 108, 110–111

FADSS. *See* Florida Association of District School Superintendents
FAPE. *See* Free Appropriate Public Education
FCAT, 33–34
federal constitutional cases: *Cook v. Stewart*, 31, 33–34, 36, 42n25; equal protection claims, 35–36; Fourteenth Amendment, 24, 24–25; substantive due process challenge, 34–35; VAMs, 31–36
final and binding arbitration, 65
"First to the Top Act," 31
Florida: administrative level hearings in, 56–58; teacher evaluation requirements in, 52–58, 61n29
Florida Association of District School Superintendents (FADSS), 102
Florida Division of Administrative Hearings, 56
Florida legislature amendments, VAMs and, 101–102
Fourteenth Amendment, 24, 24–25; equal protection clause of, 25–26; procedural due process in, 26–27; substantive due process in, 26, 27
Free Appropriate Public Education (FAPE), 110
full policy implementation delay, by litigation, 99
fundamental right, 27, 28

GAO. *See* U. S. Government Accountability Office
General Electric (GE), annual reviews of, 109–110
governance, schools sharing, 80
government separation of powers, 95
Gulfstream School, 57

HB 7069. *See* House Bill 7069
high-stakes accountability, 77–78; VAMs and, xii
"high-stakes" decisions, x, xivn6
high-stakes policy debate, courts role in, 98–99

INDEX

high-stakes testing policy litigation, courts and, 96
House Bill 7069 (HB 7069), 101
Houston Federation of Teachers v. Houston Independent School District, 38

IBB. *See* interest-based bargaining
IDEA. *See* Individuals with Disabilities Education Act
IMPACT evaluation system, 63, 69–70
individualized test scores, teacher employment decisions and, 24, 37, 41n7
Individuals with Disabilities Education Act (IDEA), 81, 110
"industrial injustice," 68
inputs, 109
Instructional Performance Evaluation and Growth Systems (IPEGS), 57–58
interest-based bargaining (IBB), xii, xvii, 79, 83; as joint problem-solving opportunity, 84; methods to, 83–84; PAR negotiation by, 84–85; traditional, 83–84
IPEGS. *See* Instructional Performance Evaluation and Growth Systems

Johnson, Barbara, 50–52
Johnson v. Francis Howell R-3 Board of Education, 48, 50–52

labor law, public sector, paradox of, 72
Lederman, Dr. Sheri, xv–xvi, xviii
Legg, John, 102
legislature amendments: HB 7069, 101; SB 736, 100–103; SB 1644, 101
litigation, 108, 112n1; compromise and, 99; full policy implementation delay by, 99; high-stakes testing policy, 96; impact of, 98; value of, 98–99
local school officials, day-to-day management to, 46–48, 59n6

malpractice, educational, ix
mandatory subject of bargaining, 65, 66
Massachusetts, educator evaluation requirement by, 18

Miami-Dade County School Board v. Hannibal Rosa, 56–57
Minnesota Supreme Court, 49
motivation, 81

national origin, religion and, 25–26
NCLB. *See* No Child Left Behind
New York legislature amendments, VAMs and, 103
New York state law constitutional cases, 39–40
No Child Left Behind (NCLB), 16, 16–17, 96, 97, 105n12, 110, 113n4
novice teachers, higher needs students with, 82

out-of-school variable, in student performance, 6, 12n33
outputs, 109

PAR. *See* peer-assisted review
peer-assisted review (PAR), xii, xvii, 79; instructional feedback by, 85; local educators and, 85; negotiation by IBB, 84–85; in personnel decisions, 85
permissive subject of bargaining, 65, 66, 74n11
PLCs. *See* professional learning communities
Policy Paradox, xvii–xviii
Pontiac v. Secretary of Education, 96–97, 98, 105n12
poverty effects, on teachers' ratings, 39
private sector, 109–110
procedural due process, in Fourteenth Amendment, 26–27
procedural violations, 71
production-function model, 2–3
professional learning communities (PLCs), 78, 83, 87, 89n10, 89n11; collaboration in, 81; school culture with, 80–81; VAMs threat to, 80–19
prohibited subject of bargaining, 65, 66
public education policy, business model transfer to, 109–110
"public" forums, 81
public school origins, states constitutions in, 46–48
public sector labor law, paradox of, 72

race: equal protection clause and, 25–26; religion and, 25–26; in student achievement, 7
Race to the Top Fund (RttT), 16, 17, 18, 103, 110
randomization, 5–6
rational basis test, 28, 34, 41n16
reduction in force (RIF), ineffective teachers and, 15
religion, national origin and, 25–26
Rhee, Michelle, 63, 69–70, 75n26
RIF. *See* reduction in force
Rosa, Hannibal, 57–58
Rose v. Council for Better Education, 39
RttT. *See* Race to the Top Fund

San Antonio Independent School District v. Rodriguez, 23–24, 26, 30, 39–40, 41n2
SB 736. *See* Senate Bill 736
SB 1644. *See* Senate Bill 1644
Scheelhaase v. Woodbury Central Community School District, 24, 29–31
school administrators, solutions for, 93
school boards, employment negotiation in, 64
School Committee of Danvers v. Tyman, 71, 76n38
school culture: attributes of, 79–80; healthy, 79; with PLCs, 80–81; student achievement and, 79–81, 90n14; VAMs and, xii, xvii; VAMs negative impact on, 81–83, 91n28
school district authority origins, personnel decisions and, 46–52
school district personnel decisions, court deference to, 48
Scott, Rick, 100, 101
Senate Bill 736 (SB 736), 100; *Cook v. Stewart* and, 101; legislature amendments to, 101–103
Senate Bill 1644 (SB 1644), 101
Sherrod v. Palm Beach County School Board, 53–55, 57, 61n38
St. Louis Teachers' Union v. Board of Education of the City of St. Louis, 24, 28–29
standardized tests: accountability emphasis on, 15–17; cheating on, 77; inflation of, 77; parent interest groups opposition to, 102; pre-VAM cases involving, 48–52; student success and, 15–16; teacher dismissal and, 45–46; teacher effectiveness and, 3, 4, 4–5, 8, 11n19; teacher evaluation using, 29–31; in VAMs, 8–9
Stanford Achievement Test, 56, 58
state law constitutions, 38–40; New York cases, 39–40; in public school origins, 46–48; teacher evaluation systems, violation of, 39–40
state legislature on, CBA, 65
state-mandated tests, teacher evaluation and student achievement on, 17, 21n9
state tenure, ineffective teachers and, 15
Stewart v. New Mexico Public Education Department, 39
Stone, Deborah, xvii–xviii
student achievement: definition of, 17; low-performing students in, 7; race in, 7; resources available in, 7; school culture and, 79–81, 90n14; school leaders in, 7; student demographics in, 6; in teacher evaluation, 18; teacher impact on, x, 2, 9n3
student demographics, in student achievement, 6
student growth, definition of, 17
student performance, out-of-school variable in, 6, 12n33
Student Success Act, 36
"substantial evidence," 49–50, 52
substantive due process: challenge, 34–35; federal constitutional cases and, 34–35; in Fourteenth Amendment, 26, 27

Taylor v. Haslam, 37
TCAP. *See* Tennessee Comprehensive Assessment Program
teacher dismissal, x, xiiin4, 71, 85; standardized tests and, 45–46
teacher employment, individualized test scores and, 24, 37, 41n7
teacher evaluation systems: of CBA, 66; employment decisions in, 19; fairness of, 80; Florida requirements of, 52–58, 61n29; pre-VAM cases in, 28–31; redesign of, ix–x, xiiin2, 16; salary adjustments in, 19; using standardized

INDEX

tests, 29–31; VAM score misuse and, 38, 43n48, 43n49. *See also* professional learning communities
teacher performance, pre-VAM cases involving, 48–52
teachers: effective, 17; liberty or property rights threatened, 27, 41n15; novice, 82; performance-based termination of, 45–46; on problem-solve issues, 80; students, responsibility of, 79–80; teaching assignments, 80; veteran, 82
teachers' ratings, poverty effects on, 39
teaching assignments, difficult, 80
teaching morale, 108
Tennessee Comprehensive Assessment Program (TCAP), 31, 32
Tennessee legislature amendments, VAMs and, 102–103
Tennessee Value-Added Assessment System (TVAAS), 18, 21n21, 31–32
tenure statutes, 47–48, 60n11
termination. *See* dismissal, of teacher
tests. *See* individualized test scores; standardized tests; state-mandated tests
Texas's state school finance formula, 23, 26
tracking, 6
traditional bargaining, 83–84
Trout v. Knox County Board of Education, 37
TVAAS. *See* Tennessee Value-Added Assessment System

U. S. Government Accountability Office (GAO), on standardized test cheating, 77
unions: collective bargaining and, 66; employment negotiation, 64; policy matter exclusions and, 67
Urbanski v. King, 39–40

validity, 5–6
value-added (VA), 2
value-added analysis (VAA), 2
value-added assessments (VAAs), 2
value-added measurement, 2
value-added models (VAMs), 2; on CBA, 66–67, 74n14, 74n15, 74n16; in collective bargaining, xvii; consequences of, xi; cost implementation of, 108, 112n1; CT ratings by, 86–87; disciplinary origins of, 2; district case complication by, 46; in employment, x–xi, 45; employment consequences and, 93, 104n2; federal constitutional cases, 31–36; in Florida, 100; Florida legislature amendments and, 101–102; Florida representative in, 100; forms of, 2; future of, 19, 22n28; high-stakes accountability and, xii; illegal collective bargaining and, 91n34; interpretation in, 3–4; in law and policy evaluation, xii; legal cases and, xi–xii, xivn11; legal mandate removal of, xviii, xxn10; legal requirement of, 46; New York legislature amendments and, 103; performance-based termination and, xi–xii; PLCs threatened by, 80–19; practical implications of, xi; reduction of, 111; reliability/stability of, 7; required use of, 86–87; school culture and, xii, xvii, 81–83, 91n28; school subject disciplines balkanization by, 82; standardized test emphasis in, 8–9; student achievement, teacher impact on, x; student success and, 78; teacher dismissal and, x, xiiin4, 71, 85; teacher evaluation systems and, 28–31, 38, 43n48, 43n49; teacher quality improvement in, 8; technical issues regarding, 4–5; Tennessee legislature amendments and, 102–103; turnover rate increase by, 82; workplace injustice and, 82
value-added score system, 18
VAMs. *See* value-added models
"vanilla" policy dispute, 112
Vergara, Beatriz, 15
Vergara v. California, 39
Vergara v. State, 15–16
veteran teachers, less needy students with, 82

Wagner v. Haslam, xvii, 24
Washington, DC, arbitration in employment decisions, 69–70
Whaley, Gerald, 48–50, 52

Whaley v. Anoka-Hennepin Independent School District, 48, 48–50, 52
workplace injustice, VAMs and, 82
workplace issues, arbitration and, 68–69
workplace stability, CBA and, 64–65

Young v. Palm Beach County Board of Education, 53, 55

ABOUT THE AUTHOR

Mark A. Paige is assistant professor of public policy at the University of Massachusetts–Dartmouth. Prior to becoming a professor, he was a school law attorney representing school districts in labor and employment and special education. He has published numerous articles on the topics of education policy and law with a particular focus on labor and employment. He received both his law degree (JD), with honors, and PhD from the University of Wisconsin–Madison.